Praise for "Writing Books for Fun, Fame & Fortune!"

"Congratulations on your delightful book on book writing. Valuable and very nicely done."
~ **Dan Poynter** / Author: **The Self-Publishing Manual - 16th Edition**

"Finally, a book that tells writers how to create a nonfiction book that gets results. It takes you step-by-creative step through an otherwise circuitous process; resulting in a book you will be proud to call your own."
~ **Brian Jud** / Author of *How to Make Real Money Selling Books* and *Beyond the Bookstore*

"As an author with several books under my belt from big publishing houses, I opened Rik Feeney's latest work with no small amount of skepticism. What could I possibly learn? And then I read it all the way to the end in one sitting. The book business is in a state of almost daily upheaval, and Rik Feeney has taken lessons from the past, melded them with contemporary market realities, and applied all of that to what we might expect in the future. In addition to being a masterful communicator who writes with great clarity and abiding good humor, Feeney arms writers with all the weapons they need for success, from methodology and nuts 'n bolts writing tools, to savvy wisdom about marketing. It's clear that Feeney had lots of fun writing this book. Here's hoping it brings fame and fortune to him and everyone who reads it."
~ **Bob Morris** / Author of *Deadly Silver Sea, Baja Florida*

"Rik Feeney's *Writing Books for Fun, Fame & Fortune* is the perfect intro guide to writing. It's clear, concise, and packed with solid advice for writing and marketing the author and his/her work. This slim book will provide you with a solid writing and publishing foundation. Crack it open and see what a gem it really is."
~ **Carol O'Dell** / Author of *Mothering Mother: A Daughter's Humorous and Heartbreaking Memoir*

"If you're even thinking about writing a book, the simple advice and methodologies in this book will help you get started, then get it done. Need some motivation and guidance? Here it is."
~ **Jim Kukral** / Author: *Internet Marketing for Business Answers - Small Business Expert Interviews*

"As a writer and editor I have read volumes about how to put a book together, and without question, Rik Feeney's "Writing Books for Fun, Fame & Fortune!" is one of the best I've come across."
~ **Chris Angermann** / **President - Florida Publisher's Association**

D1155283

"Feeney's experience as a prolific writer and book coach provide plenty of entertaining anecdotes to illustrate his easy-to-follow plan that shows anyone, from novice writer to professional, how to go from concept to published book in a matter of weeks. No excuses. If you've ever wanted to be an author, Rik Feeney shows you how."
~ D.A. Bloodsworth / Pulitzer nominee reporter and author

"A coach by nature, training and experience, Rik's step by step approaches to transforming ideas into books, articles, newsletters and novels that will sell spells sure-fire success. Rarely do fun, motivation and instruction come so neatly put together in one reference book, but that's exactly what Rik Feeney has done with this book."
~ Nancy Quatrano / Author / Copywriter / Ghostwriter

"Rik urges people to write from their passion. Without over-simplifying what's involved, he creates a road map that virtually anyone can follow. He's invariably funny, supportive, and practical in the advice he offers. Rik also offers a variety of writing and publishing resources, explanations, and suggestions that you'll seldom find all wrapped up in a single, unassuming volume."
~ Maureen A. Jung / Editor / www.wordspringconsulting.com

"In his new book, *Writing Books for Fun, Fame & Fortune*, author Rik Feeney helps get writers started on the basics before they sabotage themselves with worry about agents, publishers, royalties, advances, and such. Using Feeney's approach, writers will have most of the book already written before they even realize it. This book provides a technique that will override resistance – also known as writer's block – to the daunting task of putting your expertise into words and developing a book. *Writing Books for Fun, Fame & Fortune* is an excellent resource for helping new nonfiction writers become future experts in their areas of interest.
~ Leslie C. Halpern / Suite101®.com /Author of **Passionate About Their Work: 151 Celebrities, Artists, and Experts on Creativity**

"*Writing Books for Fun, Fame & Fortune!* is the answer to every writer's need for a blueprint. This book does not overwhelm the reader. Instead it hands the reader/writer the necessary tools to successfully complete a manuscript. One of the great values in this book is the ability to use the information over and over. Everyone who aspires to write a book should check this out!"
~ Michael Ray King / **Author: **Writing Is Easy

"Using the guidelines in Rik's book, I cannot believe I'm actually halfway through writing my first book, after a lifetime of procrastination! Great book. Highly recommend."
~ Jan Green / editor / www.thewordverve.com

Writing Books for Fun, Fame & Fortune!

RIK FEENEY

Richardson Publishing, Altamonte Springs, FL

Writing Books for Fun, Fame, & Fortune!
by Rik Feeney

ISBN: 978-1-935683-15-5

PublishingSuccessOnline.com
A division of Richardson Publishing, Inc.
PO Box 162115
Altamonte Springs, FL 32716

rik@publishingsuccessonline.com
www.PublishingSuccessOnline.com

Disclaimer:

Editorial:
Maureen Jung - http://wordspringconsulting.com/
Jennifer Gregory - jenniferediting@gmail.com
Jan Green - http://www.thewordverve.com/
Misty Powell - mysti5d@gmail.com

Cover design:
Rik Feeney – http://www.PublishingSuccessOnline.com

Cover photographs:
© c-foto |BigStockPhoto.com
© morganlstudios |BigStockPhoto.com
© InvisibleViva |BigStockPhoto.com
© blueskies9 |BigStockPhoto.com
© Franck Boston |BigStockPhoto.com
© yanc |BigStockPhoto.com

Contents:

Dedication

To the woman I will call my wife.
(Isn't it about time you let me know who you are?)

Foreword

A non-fiction book should solve a problem, relieve someone else's pain, or provide information on how to improve your life. Rik Feeney's book, *Writing Books for Fun, Fame & Fortune!* does all three. It shows you how you can easily write a book, release the hounds of creativity battling for expression, and establish you as an authority in your area of interest or passion.

Rik removes the "overwhelm" factor many new authors experience by creating a basic system of writing that allows the author to freely express him/herself in an organic (write what is foremost in your mind) rather than a linear (from beginning to end) style, the latter being the underlying cause in many cases of writer's block.

The key is to focus on the basics of book writing. Forget about publishers, agents, and especially editors. Capture the inspirational moments that occur every day and get your ideas down in a simple system that allows you to fully express yourself. In an easy-to-read and humorous style, Rik will show you how to outline and write the first draft of your book within forty days.

Rik includes several alternate forms of producing a book for those authors with great ideas, but neither the time nor the inclination to sit down and write.

Just as an athlete who dreams of Olympic glory must first master the basics, Rik has you focus on mastering the basics of writing to produce your first draft, and then once it is done, streamline the finished book with appropriate editing.

When I first wrote *The Self-Publishing Manual*, there was no Internet, no Amazon.com, or any form of electronic publishing. Today, the book industry is experiencing major advancements nearly every day. It is so much easier for you to get published than ever before. Make sure your book is a quality product by reading and using *Writing Books for Fun, Fame & Fortune!* first.

This is a great book for moms, future experts, and problem-solvers; a must for coaches, consultants, and speakers.

Is there a book inside you? I'll bet there is and I look forward to seeing it in print.

Dan Poynter
The Self-Publishing Manual
http://ParaPublishing.com

Introduction

Sometimes ignorance is truly bliss.

That's especially true when writing a book.

If I sat you down and went over all the elements needed to write a book and eventually publish it, that task would seem insurmountable and quite likely you would never make the effort.

And the rest of the world would lose the unique, funny, inspiring, or educational expertise, words of comfort, or simple advice you have to offer.

I am here to make sure that does not happen.

I believe you can write a book if you have two things: persistence and determination.

That's all it takes.

Oops! I did forget one thing: **emotion**.

What you are going to do is turn emotion into English with a very simple and easy-to-use method I call the "Top-10 Writing System."

You see, I believe we are all experts at something. I have been a gymnastics coach for over thirty years, so I certainly have some expertise in that sport. I have written over 48 books, and I am the leader of the Orlando Florida Writer's Association writing group, so I can claim some expertise in writing and publishing. I have been an avid photographer for years with photographs published in books, newspapers, and magazines that's yet another area of expertise.

If I really took the time to review my various skill sets, hobbies, and interests, I'm sure I could find several other areas of knowledge others might find useful.

You can too!

Think of the various jobs you've held during your lifetime or think about what you do right now. You know something others outside the field or those just getting started would like to know.

What are your hobbies? What are you really passionate about in life? What unique life experiences have you had that others can learn from?

"Writing is easy. All you have to do is cross out the wrong words."

- Mark Twain

Part 1: Writing A Nonfiction Book

Write a nonfiction book

I am going to help you take that experience or information and turn it into a nonfiction book!

Nonfiction?

Yes, nonfiction.

Why are fiction writers so skinny?

For those of you who write fiction, I am going to save you from years of eating Ramen noodles, while you wait for a postal employee to show up with a publishing agreement.

I am going to show you how to finance your fiction writing addiction by publishing nonfiction.

Just as your life experience has given you unique knowledge, the fiction stories you write likely require a good deal of research on particular topics. You can turn this research into nonfiction books that help pay the bills while you wait to be interviewed by Oprah.

The key to writing these nonfiction books is emotion or rather turning emotion into English using my simple 10-step system.

The burning question is, *What really pushes your buttons emotionally?* (or what pushes the buttons of others).

Actually, I should clarify that question. *What really pushes your buttons emotionally about...?* and you fill in the blank 10 times. **These Top-10 questions will become the working titles for each chapter of your book.**

Example

When I wrote the book *Gymnastics: A Guide for Parents and Athletes*, I asked the question, **What really pushes my buttons emotionally about parents of gymnasts?** Following are the answers I wrote down.

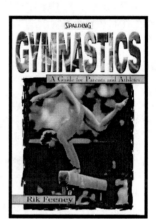

1. Why do parents ask so many questions?

2. Why don't parents understand that getting to class on time is critical for the gymnast's progression?

3. Do parents understand the gymnastics levels and why each gymnast needs to start in a basic-level class to learn foundational skills?

4. Why don't parents understand basic safety concerns in the sport of gymnastics?

5. Do parents understand the commitment necessary by both parents and gymnasts to make it to the highest levels in the sport?

6. Why do parents spread rumors when they don't understand what is happening on the gym floor?

7. Do parents understand that winning in competition is only part of the gymnastics experience?

8. How can parents, athletes, and coaches have a more harmonious experience?

9. Have the gymnast's parents considered that college green may be a better goal than Olympic gold?

10. What should parents do when the child is ready to move on to another activity?

Each of those 10 questions became working titles[1] for the chapters in my book. Before I go too far let me clarify that you can use any strong emotion to help you identify the 10 topic areas for your book.

For example:

- *What are the Top-10 things every woman should know or ask about when getting her car fixed?*

- *What are the Top-10 questions you should ask your doctor before undergoing surgery?*

- *What are 10 unique ways to create a quilt?*

- *What are the Top-10 ways to advertise free?*

- *How do you eat spaghetti with a spoon? (Top-10 ways?)*

Start your book right now

1. Pick a topic you are passionate about. The topic can be from any aspect of your life (work, play, hobby, experience, etc.).

2. Get yourself a nice pen and a set of 3X5-inch ruled index cards to keep with you day and night–even when you take a shower!

---

[1] A working title is a title used at the beginning of the writing project. As the book progresses, I might come up with a better title and replace it or it may become the final chapter title if it still works when the book is ready to go to publication.

14

3. Ideas about your topic will come to you at the oddest moments and it is your job to capture them – one idea per index card.

4. If for some reason you forget your cards or lose your pen, call your home phone and leave the idea as a voicemail message or use the voice recorder on your cell phone to capture the idea.

5. You may find the ideas coming in a mad rush, or you may start slow and collect the ideas over a few weeks, but the more you practice capturing these "aha!" moments the more frequent they will be. You will have primed your creativity pump, so to speak.

But first...

Start by writing down the 10 most important thoughts, ideas, concerns, or feelings you have about your chosen topic. The ideas you capture later on with the 3X5 cards can be sorted into the initial 10 categories of questions (chapter titles) to become a basic outline for your book.

Why the Top-10 questions?

I chose the number 10 because it seems to me everyone likes Top-10 lists. Everywhere you look, from David Letterman to *USA Today* you see Top-10 lists of likes and dislikes.[2]

Choose the 10 most important things you want someone to know about your topic.

---

[2] Hint: With all these Top-10 lists around, you may have a treasure trove of books already set to write using those lists as chapter titles.

- What questions are you asked most often (about your job, your experience, your hobby, or your passion)?

- Who most needs to know the answer (age, sex, race, education, income, job, geographic area, or physical shape)? Describe this group of potential readers, aka "your market".

- What difference will the knowledge make to your reader? What are the benefits your book will deliver?

- What are the drawbacks? What will they miss if they don't read your book?

- What pain will the message in your book relieve?

- What solution will your book provide?

Choose the number of chapter titles that fits the needs of your topic.

If you can adequately cover your topic in four chapters, then only have four chapters. If you need 16 chapters to cover the topic, use 16 chapters.

Once you have decided on the Top-10 questions (more or less), write down each question on an index card-one question per card.

Clear the table...

Next, clear off a spot on your table or on the living room carpet and place the 10 index cards in a line left to right. The order does not matter right now.

Under each index card (your chapter titles), place four more index cards. Your job is to think up four "Supporting Points" or ideas for each chapter title.

The Supporting Points may come from ideas you have already jotted down on the 3X5 cards you have captured ideas on over the past week or two or from ideas that pop into your head as you align these Supporting Points.

When you are done, pat yourself on the back, because you have just created the basic outline for your nonfiction book. (See a book outline example *Advertise for Free!* on page 22.)

In the book outline example, *Advertise for Free!* I only needed eight chapters to cover my topic. Under each chapter title, I listed four Supporting Points, shortened somewhat to fit in the tiny boxes for this example. You, however, will have the luxury of using your whole index card to state your Supporting Point.

Please, write only one idea per index card.

Why?

Limiting yourself to one idea per index card allows you to move your ideas from chapter to chapter easily, as you will likely refine your book layout several times. In addition, one idea may be relevant to more than one chapter, in which case you can make a duplicate of that card and place it where it is needed.

Release the hounds! (of creativity)

You are ready to start writing your book!

Grab a large bulletin board and pin up your cards with the chapter titles across the top and their respective Supporting Points below.[3]

The "Magic" of the Top-10 Writing System

The magic of the Top-10 Writing System is that each day you can pick any Supporting Point and write two pages or about 500 words on that topic.

One morning you may wake up and throw a dart at your board and find that day you will be writing on Chapter five, Supporting Point number three. The next day the dart lands on Chapter eight, Supporting Point number one, so you write 250 to 500 words on that topic.

But wait...

Let's say you just don't feel like tackling the subject of that Supporting Point on that day. Here's the magic: You don't have to! You can write on another Supporting Point. Write what feels right for you that day. The key to this system is that it is organic, not linear.

Linear versus Organic (choke!)

When you set out to write something the length of a book from beginning to end, your chances of reaching a choke point in the middle are staggering. Trying to make everything progress from

---

[3] You can also buy plastic business card sleeves that fit inside a three-ring binder. Simply transfer your chapter titles and Supporting Points on to the blank side of the business card. Insert the chapter titles into the tops of the card sleeves, which will leave you four blank slots under each title to insert the Supporting Point's cards. You now have a portable outline for your book!

your original premise and still reach the end goal in the coming chapters, can fry your brain as you try keeping all your ideas in coherent order.

Solution: Don't even try.

Simply write each Supporting Point as an independent piece. Write until you have fully covered the concept of the Supporting Point. When you finish your first draft of every Supporting Point of every chapter, you are then ready to refine each element to fit into one coherent whole.

Kill your editor!

By that, I mean your internal editor. The first draft of your book is your chance to explore all sorts of ideas and writing styles. There is no place for an editor while writing your first draft.

The editor's place in the process is secure when it comes time to review and revise what you have written.

I'm serious. Kill your editor!

If you use Microsoft Word and see those green and red lines under words indicating spelling errors or questionable grammar, go into the toolbar and turn off the spell checker and grammar checker or, like everyone else, you won't be able to resist correcting misspellings or trying to write a better sentence. That is editing, not creating!

Turn off your monitor!

If you can't keep yourself from correcting errors, then turn off your monitor! You don't need to see your screen to type freely and turn your emotion into creative English text.

Write with abandon. Explore your ideas without restrictions. There will be more than enough time for editing and revision in the future, I guarantee it![4]

Undue influence?

While I have extolled the virtues of creativity in writing, some fellow scribes have approached me asking for a simple system for developing the Supporting Points.

So, I stole the basic system I learned in a journalism lecture. In each Supporting Point, you will:

- Tell your reader what you are going to tell them. *(Introduction)*
- Tell them. *(Information)*
- Tell your reader what you told them. *(Summary)*

In an alternate universe...

"Khan!"

Sorry, I couldn't resist doing a William Shatner impersonation or making a Star Trek reference.

In another universe, you could simply focus your Supporting Points on:

- The Problem
- The Solution
- The Benefit

---

[4] When you do get to the editing process, make it a habit to keep everything that you remove, which may later turn into separate articles, blog posts, or ideas for other books.

Or, for you dyed-in-the-wool fiction writers:

- Complication
- Crisis
- Resolution

And, yes, you can use dramatic, fiction-writing techniques in developing a nonfiction book.

See the template *Supporting Idea Development Outline* on page 23 for help developing your Supporting Points.[5]

Let's do the math

If you have kept up with the steps already outlined, you now have 10 chapter ideas and four Supporting Points for each chapter.[6]

Your goal is to write approximately two pages or 500 words on one of your Supporting Points each day. Understand that 500 words is an arbitrary goal. You may need to write 1,000 words on a particular subject, or you may only need 250 words. Simply write until you have adequately covered the topic, then move on.

Remember, you can write your chapters and Supporting Points in any order. Write what feels right for you for each day.

If you have 10 chapters and write two pages for each Supporting Point each day (a total of 80 pages), it will take you 40 days to write the first draft of your book.

---

[5] Remember, this is one idea how to do it, not the end-all-be-all answer. Do what works best for you.
[6] Remember: The number of chapters and Supporting Points will vary. Create as many or as few as you need to effectively cover your subject.

You are the expert

Remember, you are the expert. Your employment, life experience, hobbies, and much more have already given you a wealth of knowledge. Write about what you know. Your opinion or your thoughts can help other people.

Don't get caught up in the idea that you need to research extensively. If necessary, read just enough to make your topic viable for your current needs, but focus mainly on expressing your own thoughts, rather than regurgitating the ideas of others.

Believe and achieve

I believe everyone has a book inside him or her that can benefit others. So, the bottom line is, "If you believe you can write a book, you can write a book." Print out your daily goal of writing and place the pages in a three-ring binder, so you can watch your book become a reality day by day.

Imagine this: In the very near future, you can say with pride that you are a published author.

Special Note: On page 24, I have included a copy of a blank template titled, ***Non-Fiction Storyboard.*** Make copies of this template and carry them with you to jot down an outline for another book while you are waiting in line at the store, stuck in traffic, or when you feel the need to capture a brilliant idea. To give you enough room to write, I only included eight chapter sections on this page. You can use all eight, only four, or, if you need more chapter sections, simply make more copies and re-number the sections. ***Go for it!***

But, what if I can't write?

So what?

The most important thing is you have a solution to someone else's problem. (More on that in a moment.)

Right now, the most important thing you can do is to write down your ideas in the format I present in this book.

Don't cop out!

Do your best to put the ideas in your own words, but don't get hung up over grammar, punctuation, spelling, or even your author's voice (how you come across in writing).

When you are finished recording your thoughts and ideas, you can hire (or trade services with someone) an editor, ghostwriter, or book doctor to clean up your manuscript.

I'll try, but...

"I'll try, but..." is the sentence everyone uses as an excuse for failure in advance.

Don't even think you can get away with that with me!

As Yoda, the Jedi master said to Luke Skywalker, "Try? There is no try. There is only do or do not."

Words to live by.

The big BUT

Whenever I hear the word "but" tacked on after the phrase "I'll try," I know I am going to hear an excuse for failure in advance.

"I'll try, but I think I'm having a baby that week."

"I'll try, but I'm all out of clean underwear. I only have my emergency granny panties left and I was saving them for a special occasion."

"I'll try, but my proctologist has scheduled me for brain surgery that week."

Ridiculous? Maybe, but I have heard some bizarre excuses.

The bottom line

You can make an excuse or you can make an effort. The result from the former is a lot of hot air, the result from the latter is a document you can develop into a saleable book.

Keep in mind that this is not rocket surgery.

You are simply writing down some unique ideas, experiences, or guidelines that could help someone else.

In fact, the basics of marketing a nonfiction book are:

1. Identify a pain or problem (common to a large group of people).

2. Develop a solution and write it down in a book (like you are learning to do here!).
3. Sell your book with the solution for a good profit.
4. Rinse and repeat.

Pain trumps pleasure

To forestall any complaints from the glass is half-full side of the literary world, the reality is that people will do more to keep from losing something or to relieve a pain, than they will to achieve a higher goal or improve their health.

Most of us live in a "comfort zone" and can only be relied upon to act accordingly when we believe we are about to lose something.

You are going to lose

As a person with a fertile and active imagination, you stand to lose hundreds or even thousands of dollars in income if you continue to make excuses like, "I'll try, but I'm not sure I can write."

Just give it your best shot. The final document can be cleaned up later. And, if you talk to any ghostwriter, he or she will tell you it is infinitely easier to work from a written document than it is to create from whole cloth.

This subject is closed.

Now, write your book!

Non-Fiction Storyboard / Working Title: Advertise for Free!

Chapter 1 Title	Chapter 2 Title	Chapter 3 Title	Chapter 4 Title	Chapter 5 Title	Chapter 6 Title	Chapter 7 Title	Chapter 8 Title
Marketing, Public Relations & Advertising	A.I.D.A.	Mining Your Own "Acres of Diamonds"	Free Ways to Advertise	The Media Release	Brochures, Business Cards, & Flyers	Your Web Site	Television & Radio
Supporting Point #1	Supporting Point #1	Supporting Point #1	Supporting Point #1	Supporting Point #1	Supporting Point #1	Supporting Point #1	Supporting Point #1
What is Marketing?	Attention	Customer Information	Word of Mouth	Formatting Correctly	Developing the Brochure	Domain Registry	Start Local: Expand to Regional & National
Supporting Point #2	Supporting Point #2	Supporting Point #2	Supporting Point #2	Supporting Point #2	Supporting Point #2	Supporting Point #2	Supporting Point #2
What is Public Relations?	Interest	Capturing E-mails	E-mail	WII-FM Content	Business Card Savvy	Developing The Site	Looking and Sounding Good
Supporting Point #3	Supporting Point #3	Supporting Point #3	Supporting Point #3	Supporting Point #3	Supporting Point #3	Supporting Point #3	Supporting Point #3
What is Advertising?	Desire	Referrals	Free Articles & Reports	Targeting Specific Media	Flashy Flyers	Search Engine Optimize	Contacting Producers
Supporting Point #4	Supporting Point #4	Supporting Point #4	Supporting Point #4	Supporting Point #4	Supporting Point #4	Supporting Point #4	Supporting Point #4
Consistency: Key to Successful Results	Action	Upgrading, Adding, Simplifying	Parking Around Town	Follow up & Thank you	Looking Good In Print	Show Me The Money!	Online, PDF, & Print Media Kits

Non-Fiction Storyboard / Support Idea Development Outline

Chapter #	Support Idea #

Tell them what you are going to tell them.

WHAT?

(A brief description of supporting idea, experience, information, or opinion.)

HOW? **WHY?** **WHERE?** **WHEN?** **WHO?**

Tell them! Use descriptive words, develop mental pictures, tug the reader's emotions.

<u>Body of the message:</u> 3-4 supporting points of information for the above idea, experience, information, or opinion.

Tell them what you told them.

<u>Summary:</u> In one short paragraph summarize what you just told them.

Non-Fiction Storyboard / Working Title: _____   Date: _____

Chapter 1 Title	Chapter 2 Title	Chapter 3 Title	Chapter 4 Title	Chapter 5 Title	Chapter 6 Title	Chapter 7 Title	Chapter 8 Title
Supporting Point #1	Supporting Point #1	Supporting Point #1	Supporting Point #1	Supporting Point #1	Supporting Point #1	Supporting Point #1	Supporting Point #1
Supporting Point #2	Supporting Point #2	Supporting Point #2	Supporting Point #2	Supporting Point #2	Supporting Point #2	Supporting Point #2	Supporting Point #2
Supporting Point #3	Supporting Point #3	Supporting Point #3	Supporting Point #3	Supporting Point #3	Supporting Point #3	Supporting Point #3	Supporting Point #3
Supporting Point #4	Supporting Point #4	Supporting Point #4	Supporting Point #4	Supporting Point #4	Supporting Point #4	Supporting Point #4	Supporting Point #4

Part 2:

Chapter Summaries and Introduction

Congratulations!

Now that you have written your 10 questions (or chapter titles), provided four Supporting Points for each, and written 250 to 500 words for each Supporting Point (in the order of your choice), you now have completed the critical core of your book.

Let's keep the momentum and move on to the next step.

Chapter Introductions and Summaries

I have always found it a silly practice to write the introduction and the summary for a chapter before you even know what you are going to say.

As you explore each Supporting Point as an independent writing exercise, with the goal of covering the topic completely and creatively, you may find yourself exploring thoughts and ideas that are or were completely unexpected.[7]

That's what is great about organic writing. You are able to fully explore the ideas in each Supporting Point.

But now that you know what each Supporting Point in this chapter is about, you can link them together, first with your summary and then with your introduction.

By that, I mean write the chapter summary before you write the introduction.

---

[7] Sometimes ideas may come to you totally off the topic about which you are writing. Capture the "Aha!" moments by typing *** then key in the intruding thought. Bracket it with another set of three ***'s then go back to the piece you were working on. You can cut and paste these ideas into another document later, just by using the search function to look for three ***'s.

Last comes first

The chapter summary may be one paragraph to one page in length. Since it is a "summary," the idea is to condense the information from the chapter (the four Supporting Points) as briefly and as effectively as possible.

Once you finish the summaries (see page 34 for Summary Outline) you can begin work on the introductions to each chapter.

In the beginning...

Have you ever been asked to introduce someone you have never met?

What would you say?

To introduce someone appropriately, you need to know something about him or her, have some personal experience, or be able to read a prepared biography.

The same is true of the chapter you have just written. How can you write an introduction without first becoming acquainted with its content? That's why I ask you to write the introduction to each chapter last. (See page 35 for an Introduction Outline)

Storyboard with Summaries and Introductions

On page 32 you'll find a more refined version of the storyboard you used to outline your book. It contains the Top-10 questions across the top as chapter titles, with the four Supporting Points listed under each chapter title.

But now, we have added two boxes under each section for Summaries and Introductions.

One a day...

The guidelines are the same as for writing the Supporting Points. At a minimum, write a one-page summary each day for each chapter, in any order you choose.

Then, write a one-page introduction for each chapter in any order you choose.

Note: To be most effective, write the chapter summary before writing the introduction.

You may write a summary and introduction for the same chapter in one day, but always write the summary before writing the introduction.

P.S. The editor is still dead.

Keep in mind while writing summaries and introductions that these are still creative nonfiction writing pieces. Allow your inspiration to run wild without judgment or evaluation. There will be time for that later.

Have you gained weight?

Certainly not you, the author, but your book has just grown around 20 more pages. Let's do the math:

10 chapters x 1 page summary = 10 pages.

10 chapters x 1 page introduction = 10 pages.

That's a total of 20 more pages added to the 80 pages you already wrote for a total of 100 pages so far!

The end is in sight...

Now, it's time for you to start getting pretty excited, because you are almost done writing the first draft of your book.

In Part 3, you will add the summary for the whole book, then finally, write the introduction for your book.

Good job! Your persistence and determination will pay off! Count on it.

"Don't try to figure out what other people want to hear from you; figure out what you have to say. It's the one and only thing you have to offer."

- Barbara Kingsolver

Chapter Summary

Parting Words (or "Summary" or "Conclusion.")

WHAT? | Tell them what you are going to tell them.

Summary: A description that basically states, "Here's what we learned from this chapter."

WHO? WHEN? WHERE? WHY? | Tell them! Use descriptive words, develop mental pictures, tug the reader's emotions.

Body of the message: (3-4 supporting points of information for the summary.)

HOW? | Tell them what you told them.

Summary: In one or two sentences summarize what you just told them, possibly provide a sneak peek of the next chapter, and invite the reader to continue reading.

Chapter Introduction

Headline: 5-7 words that grab **ATTENTION!**

WHAT? | Tell them what you are going to tell them.

Introduction: The message objective, or what the reader **NEEDS** to know. One or two sentences stressing the **benefits, benefits, benefits** of reading this chapter.

WHO? WHEN? WHERE? WHY? | Tell them! Use descriptive words, develop mental pictures, tug the reader's emotions.

Body of the message: (3-4 supporting points of information for the introduction)

HOW? | Tell them what you told them.

Summary: In one or two sentences summarize what you just told them.

Non-Fiction Storyboard / Chapter Summaries & Introductions   Date:

Chapter 1 Title	Chapter 2 Title	Chapter 3 Title	Chapter 4 Title	Chapter 5 Title	Chapter 6 Title	Chapter 7 Title	Chapter 8 Title
Supporting Point #1	Supporting Point #1	Supporting Point #1	Supporting Point #1	Supporting Point #1	Supporting Point #1	Supporting Point #1	Supporting Point #1
Supporting Point #2	Supporting Point #2	Supporting Point #2	Supporting Point #2	Supporting Point #2	Supporting Point #2	Supporting Point #2	Supporting Point #2
Supporting Point #3	Supporting Point #3	Supporting Point #3	Supporting Point #3	Supporting Point #3	Supporting Point #3	Supporting Point #3	Supporting Point #3
Supporting Point #4	Supporting Point #4	Supporting Point #4	Supporting Point #4	Supporting Point #4	Supporting Point #4	Supporting Point #4	Supporting Point #4
Introduction Chapter 1	Introduction Chapter 2	Introduction Chapter 3	Introduction Chapter 4	Introduction Chapter 5	Introduction Chapter 6	Introduction Chapter 7	Introduction Chapter 8
Summary Chapter 1	Summary Chapter 2	Summary Chapter 3	Summary Chapter 4	Summary Chapter 5	Summary Chapter 6	Summary Chapter 7	Summary Chapter 8

Part 3: Book Summary and Introduction

Book Summary & Introduction

Another storyboard?

Yup! It's time to update your storyboard again by adding a summary for your whole book and the introduction to the whole book. (see page 42)

What comes first...

Just as in writing your chapters, writing the summary for the book comes before writing the introduction for the whole book.

The book summary

Now that you know what your book is about, you are ready to write the summary. In effect, you will take a soup bowl of information and condense it down to a bouillon cube's worth of knowledge. (see page 43)

Review your chapter summaries

When writing your book summary, it will help to review each of your chapter summaries and pull out the single most-important element of each chapter.

Special Note: These 10 most-important summary elements from each chapter may form the basis of your "back copy blurb" (the information you place on the back cover to entice people to buy the book) or at least get you started on your blurb.

The book introduction

Finally, you begin with the end in mind. Literally, since you are now intimately familiar with every word in your book, you are now ready to introduce it to the world.

In the book summary, you already told everyone what you were going to tell them.

Remember the easiest way to write a book is to:

- Tell them what you are going to tell them. *(Introduction)*
- Tell them. *(Book chapters)*
- Tell them what you told them. *(Summary)*

The BIG difference...

There is a difference between the Summary and the Introduction for both the individual chapters and the book as a whole.

Any summary is more or less a straightforward retelling of the main points discussed in the chapter or book. (Remember: It can still be creative!)

In your introductions to the chapters and to the book, I suggest you present the main points with a bit of a tease, very similar to what you hear in commercials for the nightly news.

"Did the President really poke his kitten with a fork? News at eleven!"

Developing questions about each of your chapter titles that intrigue the readers will definitely make them want to read your book to find the answers. (See page 44 for Book Introduction outline.)

You've come a long way...

The biggest chunk of your book is done. The next section will deal with fleshing out the rest of your book, to make it ready for publication and promote the highest number of sales.

In the next section, you will learn how to add the back matter.

Back matter: The back matter many times consists of:

1. Appendix (appendices)

2. Glossary

3. References

4. Resources and Links

5. Bibliography

6. Index

7. About the author

8. Ordering Information

9. New book preview

You will also learn how to add the front matter.

Front Matter: The front matter many times consists of:

1. Testimonials

2. Title page

3. Publication page

Publish your book NOW!

Are you ready to publish right now but not quite sure how to do it?

I can save you, literally, thousands of dollars as your personal book coach, editor, cover designer and publishing consultant.

Your book can be published as an ebook through Kindle, a paper book via print-on-demand technologies, or developed as an audio book and sold as a CD or mp3 download.

Do you need a book cover or marketing image?

Could you use some help creating marketing descriptions that sell your book, or marketing strategies to launch your book, as well as ongoing marketing techniques for sales success?

For publishing success, go to:

www.RickFeeney.com
usabookcoach@gmail.com / 407-529-8539

4. Acknowledgments and Dedications

5. Contents page

6. Foreword (note: it is not spelled "forward")

Keep up the good work and I'll see you in the next section!

"We are all apprentices in a craft where no one ever becomes a master."

- Ernest Hemingway

Non-Fiction Storyboard with Book Summary & Book Introduction   Date:

Book Summary

Book Introduction

	Chapter 1 Title	Chapter 2 Title	Chapter 3 Title	Chapter 4 Title	Chapter 5 Title	Chapter 6 Title	Chapter 7 Title	Chapter 8 Title
	Supporting Point #1	Supporting Point #1	Supporting Point #1	Supporting Point #1	Supporting Point #1	Supporting Point #1	Supporting Point #1	Supporting Point #1
	Supporting Point #2	Supporting Point #2	Supporting Point #2	Supporting Point #2	Supporting Point #2	Supporting Point #2	Supporting Point #2	Supporting Point #2
	Supporting Point #3	Supporting Point #3	Supporting Point #3	Supporting Point #3	Supporting Point #3	Supporting Point #3	Supporting Point #3	Supporting Point #3
	Supporting Point #4	Supporting Point #4	Supporting Point #4	Supporting Point #4	Supporting Point #4	Supporting Point #4	Supporting Point #4	Supporting Point #4
	Introduction Chapter 1	Introduction Chapter 2	Introduction Chapter 3	Introduction Chapter 4	Introduction Chapter 5	Introduction Chapter 6	Introduction Chapter 7	Introduction Chapter 8
	Summary Chapter 1	Summary Chapter 2	Summary Chapter 3	Summary Chapter 4	Summary Chapter 5	Summary Chapter 6	Summary Chapter 7	Summary Chapter 8

Book Summary

Parting Words (or "Summary" or "Conclusion.")

WHAT?

Tell them what you are going to tell them.

Summary: A description that basically states, "Here's what we learned from this book."

WHO? WHEN? WHERE? WHY?

Tell them! Use descriptive words, develop mental pictures, tug the reader's emotions.

Body of the message: (3-4 supporting points of information for the summary.)

HOW?

Tell them what you told them.

Summary: In one or two sentences summarize what you just told them, say goodbye, and provide them additional information on how to contact you.

Book Introduction

Headline: 5-7 words that grab **ATTENTION!**

WHAT?

Tell them what you are going to tell them.

Introduction: The message objective, or what the reader **NEEDS** to know. One or two sentences stressing the **benefits, benefits, benefits** of reading this book.

WHO? WHEN? WHERE? WHY?

Tell them! Use descriptive words, develop mental pictures, tug the reader's emotions.

<u>Body of the message:</u> (3-4 supporting points of information for the introduction)

HOW?

Tell them what you told them.

<u>Summary:</u> In one or two sentences summarize what you just told them.

Part 4:

Front Matter and Back Matter

Front Matter and Back Matter

Back matter

Tying up loose ends

The back matter in your book can make the difference between modest and impressive book sales, especially to libraries.

The reference librarian

If you have ever gone to the library to research a subject, you may have noticed the reference librarian knows which books will be the most helpful, mainly because these books contain a great deal of reference material such as a glossary, an index, a list of works referenced, a list of resources and links, a bibliography, and an appendix.

Here are some brief descriptions of each useful section:

Appendix: A section of the book where additional information, not always directly relevant to the current work is added. An appendix may contain recipes, charts and illustrations, more technical information, etc. A book may have more than one appendix.

Glossary: A listing of terms and their definitions used in your particular area of expertise. For instance, when writing on the sport of gymnastics, I may list skills by name and description.

References and/or Bibliography: Research librarians will find your book especially useful if you include bibliographic information on any articles, books, or web sites you have referenced to write your book. As an expert, you may have needed no additional research, but it's a good idea to list a dozen or so references for additional information.

Resources and/or Links: List all the web sites you can find that have information pertinent to the topic of your book.

Index: An index that lists all subjects covered in the book, alphabetically, is great, but you may want to get a professional indexer to do this for you. It can be a time consuming job. An index is not critical, but again, it could help with library sales of your book.

About the author: A brief one to two paragraph biography of the author, including a photograph and links to the author's web site or blog.

Ordering information: Specific contact information that will guide the reader to web sites where your book is for sale or contact information to reach the book's publisher.

Front matter

Within these pages...

Besides the Title, Book cover, and the Back copy blurb, the material inside the front of the book especially the Contents page and the grab-you-by-the-throat first chapter will make the most impact on sales.

What others say...

Testimonials: Usually a two or three sentence statement extolling the virtues of your book. They can be written by family, friends, and relatives, experts, celebrities, and shivers, maybe even Oprah! Testimonials definitely help to sell a book.

Title page: Just after the testimonials is a right facing page called the title page. This page contains the title of the book, the author's name, and usually the name of the publishing company. This page does not require illustration, although it may have one.

Publication page: One of the more important pages in the book, the publication page contains the book title, author's name, copyright date, rights reserved, ISBN number, and possibly a Library of Congress number. It also includes the publisher's name and address, as well as a disclaimer relieving the author and publisher of any responsibility for material contained in the book—at least that is the theory.

The publication page may also contain Cataloging-in-Publication data, which you can learn how to develop with help from a friendly research librarian.

The bottom of the publication page usually lists credits and recognition of copyright information for photographers, illustrators, cover designers, editors, and stock photography licenses (if necessary).

Acknowledgments: This is the page where you acknowledge everyone who helped you in any way make this book a reality. From a political, and even a sales standpoint, it is best to name everyone you can along with a thousand best friends, coworkers, and relatives.

Dedication page: If you are smart, you will dedicate the book to your spouse or your mother. The only other people to consider would be those likely to put you in their will.

Contents page: The contents page is another book element critical for sales. Many people will study the contents page to get an idea of what the book is all about. The contents page should include the chapter titles as well as a listing of subheads used throughout each chapter. Done right, it will look almost like an outline for the book.

Foreword: While a foreword for a book is not a necessity, it is a great place to invite a local celebrity or expert on the subject say a few words about you, the subject, and your book. Please note that it is spelled "f-o-r-e-w-o-r-d," not "forward," which is a direction of travel readers will not take after such an egregious error on your part.

Wow, can you believe it? You are finished with the first draft of your book.

First draft?

Yes, first draft. What you need to do now is put the book in a drawer and let it sit for a week or two, so you can come back to it with fresh eyes and begin your first edit. Revision is one of the keys to quality writing.

Rik's soapbox

Print-on-Demand is a great technology allowing many people to publish quality books.

Unfortunately, the quality books make up perhaps 1 percent of the books self-published; 99percent of the books self-published are simply not yet ready for publication.

"Not ready" means they have not been professionally edited, the book covers look like my kindergarten artwork, and the interiors are not designed and paginated in a professional manner.

Intermission

What I want you to do now is put your manuscript off to the side and read the next few sections to learn about some alternate ways to produce a book.

Once you are done, you can return to the section on editing and revising and begin to write a little bit more tightly.

*"Either write something worth reading
or do something worth writing."*

- Ben Franklin

Part 5:

Alternate Ways to Write a Book

Talk your way to a book

I like to talk. In fact, if you give me a chance to bullsh*t, umm...,
chat in front of any group of people; I can be relied on to keep
them entertained for a good day or two.

Shoot, when I go to a writer's conference, I almost always tell
the director of the conference that I am available to do a talk
should some other speaker mysteriously get food poisoning
during lunch (heh, heh, heh...).

Okay, I admit to a bit of exaggeration. I don't really poison
another speaker's food (but I might slip them some chocolate
chip cookies made with chocolate-flavored ExLax).

But I digress...

The point of this section is that it may be infinitely more
comfortable for you to talk your way through a nonfiction book.

There are several ways you can do that.

Obviously, if money is not a big issue for you, you can hire a film
crew to track you day and night and record every aspect of your
life. You can then transcribe the minutiae of day-to-day life and
sell it to bird owners to paper the bottom of their pet's cage.

You could also hire a court reporter with a rolling dolly to put her
transcription thingy on and can capture the pearls of wisdom
that drip from your lips.

Wow, this bloke has turned into a smarmy little git, eh guv'nor?

Yes, Mary Poppins, he has!

Okay, I promise, no more fooling around.

The real deal

Before you have gained experience as a speaker in front of a group of people you may want to start by recording your talks through your computer.

Most computers with Windows XP, Vista, or Windows 7 have a speech recognition and recording ability. All you need to do is invest in an inexpensive USB microphone from Radio Shack and you can start speaking your book into your computer.

Audio file or transcription?

You can create a couple of different products from this file. The first could be an audio version of your book, which you can sell as an MP3 download or record to a CD, to sell from your web site, then pack and ship to the customer.

Dragon Naturally Speaking

If you want to get a little fancy, you can buy a software program titled, Dragon Naturally Speaking.

After teaching the computer to recognize your voice by reading a couple of paragraphs, you can start dictating your book and watch the words appear on the screen right before your eyes.

The digital recorder

You can record yourself giving talks on your subject of choice to local business and special interest groups and have those talks transcribed to use as the basis for your next book.

The Speaker's Game Plan

1. Determine the subject of your talk.

2. Develop a 45-minute to one-hour talk on the subject.

3. Use a small digital recorder to record the talk.

4. Use audio software like *Sony Sound Forge* to edit the talk and sell it as an audio book (CD or MP3 download).

5. Download the audio file to your computer, then send it as an attachment to a transcriber who will type it up and return it to you as a Word document,[8] which you can edit, add to, or delete from to create your final book product.

Smaller bites, please!

Okay, the first thing you need to do is decide what topic you want to talk about and/or create as a book product.

As in the previous section, I suggested you pick a subject near and dear to your heart, a subject you are passionate about, a subject with which you have personal experience, and you can easily write about without the need for extensive research.

---

[8] I use Jan Green at TheWordVerve to transcribe and edit all my audio files. Contact Jan at www.thewordverve.com

First, create a storyboard (as described in the previous section) to develop a basic outline for your talk.

Then take your outline and create a PowerPoint presentation for your audience to follow along with and take notes while you talk.

A basic outline for your talk

1. Introduction of the speaker

It's great if you can get someone else to brag on you for a few minutes, but if not, always take a few minutes to let people know who you are, how you are like them, and how you can help them. (5 minutes)

Note: Always bring a written copy of your introduction with you. You don't want somebody else getting creative or worse trying to be funny while introducing you.

Super Special Notice: Accolades are great, but if you set yourself up as being superior to your audience, they will not be able to relate to your message.

People like others who are like themselves.

Show them how you learned through mistakes you have made. It makes you seem human and likeable.

2. Introduce the talk Tell them what you are going to tell them.

Give a brief overview of your talk. Pique their interest. Promise a few salient points that will really make a difference in their lives. (5 minutes)

3. Tell them

Tell a story. Make a point. (10 minutes)
Tell a story. Make a point. (10 minutes)
Tell a story. Make a point. (10 minutes)

No, I am not stuttering nor is the needle stuck on my record player. People love stories. Tell three stories illustrating some aspect of your talk along with a powerful lesson or piece of information listeners can take home, and you will easily keep your audience captivated.

4. Tell them what you told them

In your conclusion or speech summary, tell one last story or simply summarize the points of your three main stories. (5 minutes).

5. Question and answer period

Your audience may surprise you with some valuable or insightful questions and comments that will round out your presentation (15 minutes).

Permission to record?

When recording any talk make sure the audience is aware they are being recorded for the purpose of developing a commercial product that may be transcribed and may also be sold as an audio product like an MP3 download.

If they do not wish to be on the recording or have their comments transcribed, they should hold their questions and comments until after the recording has concluded. **Note**: In a public building or at a private company, you may need to get permission to record in advance of your talk.

Collect columns, blogs, or online articles

One of the best ways to get the word out about your new book is through a blog or regular column you write online or through traditional sources.

You can also create a book by collecting those blog posts or column articles that collectively help solve a problem, relieve a pain, or possibly provide a solution to your reader's problems.

Online column

I write books on the sport of gymnastics, so I applied to **AllExperts.com** to answer questions in the category of gymnastics. I now have nearly two hundred thousand words in answers I have supplied.

I can search through all those answers and literally have several books almost already written and ready to publish, by copying and pasting articles about specific subjects into a Word document.

The column also gives me real time feedback into the current issues that concern gymnasts, coaches, and parents.

With that knowledge, I can supply special reports and books within a week or two.

The same is true for blogs and article depositories.

Blogs

Blogs or web logs are online diaries (more or less). You pick a topic and tell the world what you think about it.

If you promote your blog through family, friends, and relatives, as well as post guest blogs on other sites, you can develop a large following of readers who will provide comments and feedback. By archiving your blogs, you will soon have a large body of work to draw from and develop your book.

Article directories

If you don't want to deal with the pressure of having to write a blog on a regular basis, you can write individual articles and post each at an article directory site like **Hub Pages** or **EzineArticles.com**.[9]

Again, once you have developed an archive of articles, you may find you have enough material to develop a book.

> *"If I don't write to empty my mind,*
> *I go mad."*
>
> *- Lord Byron*

---

[9] A list of article directories can be found at http://www.vretoolbar.com/articles/directories.php.

Books via Digital Interview

Here's another great way to produce a book quick: digital interviews.

There are two distinct ways to create a book using this method.

In-person interview

I have had clients (who because of severe medical injury or illness) were unable to sit at a computer and type their stories.

So, I went to a local electronics store and bought myself a digital recorder. I happened to get an Olympus WS-110, but there are other types available.

This particular recorder could digitally record up to 67 hours when set in regular record mode, but even in the high quality mode could still record for up to 17 hours.

The quality of the recording is great. In fact, when I give talks, I always record myself using this digital recorder, and then send the audio file to my transcriptionist and have the basics of a book ready to publish after a bit of editing and cover design.

Plug it in

I absolutely adore any device that makes my life easier. This little Olympus recorder pulls apart to reveal a USB connection that I can plug into a USB port right on my computer.

The software for the recorder is built into it so the file begins to download automatically. I don't have to do anything!

Back to our bedridden book writer

With digital recorder in hand, I simply asked the writer a few questions and then sat back and let her talk for the next four hours, interjecting questions now and then for clarity, but mostly letting her tell her own story.

I then downloaded that file and sent it to a transcriptionist to be formatted into a Word file, which I then turn into a book.

Structured or off the cuff?

You can use the Top-10 Writing System to create a basic outline to follow or, if the interviewee is articulate, you can just let them tell the story as it naturally unfolds.

"A synonym is a word you use when you can't spell the other one."

- Baltasar Gracián

Digital Interview by Phone

By purchasing a **Radio Shack – Wireless Phone Recording Controller – Cat. # 17-855**, you can easily interview experts, celebrities, or persons of interest anywhere in the world via your phone.

Gymnastics Choreography – The Book

One day I decided I was going to do a book on gymnastics choreography. Having been a coach for 30-years I knew all the questions a parent new to optional competition would ask.

- *What kind of music is best?*

- *How long should the routine be?*

- *What tricks are required in my routine?*

Of course, there were several more questions, which I wrote down and then sent to one of America's top gymnastics choreographers, Kris Robinson.[10]

After giving Kris a chance to review the questions for a few days and prepare her answers, I called her on the phone and assumed the role of a parent new to the sport of gymnastics. Over the next 90-minutes, I asked her several questions about Gymnastics Choreography.

Using an inexpensive audio-editing software program called **Sony Sound Forge**; I edited the interview down to a 57-minute audio CD, which I sell on my site.[11]

---

[10] Send an email to thepostukelady@aol.com to contact Kris Robinson about choreography.

[11] www.GymnasticsTrainingTips.com

That interview is also available as an Adobe eBook, a Kindle book, a Nook book, and by the time you read this, may be available in several other formats.

Whom do you know?

What experts, celebrities, or persons of interest do you know? What information do they have that other people would like to know? Remember the six degrees of separation? You're close-really close – to someone who knows anyone you want to reach (at least Kevin Bacon). So think big...

You can easily create several new books a year interviewing experts in their area of specialty.

You will need to get permission from the expert to use their information in the book, but I think you will find many of them honored to be involved.

The final book will not only increase the expert's standing and credibility, but will also be a great promotional tool for them.

Split the Profits

If need be, you can split the profits (after expenses) between yourself and the "interviewee / author." Splitting does not necessarily mean 50-50; it could be 90-10 in your favor.

Critical Understanding:

Always remember, only 5 percent of your effort will be expended in writing and publishing your book. 95 percent of the effort goes into marketing and promoting. Keep that in mind if you decide to divvy up the profits.

The Anthology Method of Book Development

Practically everyone on the planet has heard of the *Chicken Soup for the Soul* series of books by Jack Canfield and Mark Victor Hansen. What makes these books unique, at least to me, is that a majority if not all of the books in the *Chicken Soup* series were created through article or story contributions by authors other than Jack and Mark.

Are these guys geniuses or what?

I think the only other person with that much success developing a book in a similar style is God! You know the Bible...

The kicker is you can do the same thing. Okay, maybe not the Bible but...

The basics revisited

Choose a topic that you are passionate about that will help other people solve a problem, relieve a pain, or achieve a goal. Your book is simply a pre-packaged solution to a problem.

Article directories

Search article directories online like **Hub Pages** or **EzineArticles** and collect articles that meet the needs of your topic. You can also find information via newsletters and web sites. Just remember always to ask permission first before you use the material.

New book! Mercury Madness

Suppose I was passionate about the topic of mercury poisoning, and I decided to write a book titled, *Mercury Madness: The Causes, Cures, and Controversy of Mercury Poisoning.*

I could go to an article directory like *EzineArticles* and collect all the best articles pertaining to the causes, cures, and controversy of mercury poisoning. Because each article has a bio box with the author's contact information, I can contact the author of each article for permission to include it in my book.

Sample of my bio box (attached to every article I write)

Rik Feeney is the author of the **Back Handsprings: The Secret Techniques** and several other books on the sport of gymnastics available at **www.GymnasticsTrainingTips.com**. Rik is also a Self-Publishing Coach, consulting with authors to write, publish and promote books, and develop author web sites. He has presented several talks at writer's conferences and seminars throughout the Southeast and is finishing his new book, **Writing for Fun, Fame, & Fortune.** Email Rik at **rik@publishingsuccessonline.com** or visit his web site at **www.PublishingSuccessOnline.com**.

Contact the authors

Just as you can easily contact me via the information in my "bio box" so can you contact authors of articles you think will fit within your book.

The pleasure is all mine

I think you will be pleasantly surprised by the number of authors who will jump at the chance to have one of their articles published in a book. Being published in a book is a tremendous validation of one's efforts.

In addition, it can be a great promotion of the author and his/her work, especially if you include the author's bio box within your book, along with all their contact information.

You swear to tell the truth...

For legal reasons, make sure you have the author of every article published in your book sign a release stating they have the authority to grant you the right to publish the article in your book. You may want to get some professional legal advice to develop your release.

Basic book format (using contributed articles)

Book cover with title and byline "Written and edited by..."

Front Matter:
- Testimonials page
- Title page
- Publication page
- Dedications / Acknowledgments
- Contents
- Foreword (?)

Introduction (written by you)

Section 1: Causes of Mercury Poisoning
Introduction (written by you)
- Article 1 (contributed by outside author)
- Article 2 (contributed by outside author)
- Article 3 (contributed by outside author)
- Article 4 (contributed by outside author)
- Article 5 (contributed by outside author)
- Article 6 (contributed by outside author)

Summary (written by you)

Section 2: Cures for Mercury Poisoning
Introduction (written by you)
- Article 1 (contributed by outside author)
- Article 2 (contributed by outside author)
- Article 3 (contributed by outside author)
- Article 4 (contributed by outside author)
- Article 5 (contributed by outside author)
- Article 6 (contributed by outside author)

Summary (written by you)

Section 3: Controversy surrounding Mercury Poisoning
Introduction (written by you)
- Article 1 (contributed by outside author)
- Article 2 (contributed by outside author)
- Article 3 (contributed by outside author)
- Article 4 (contributed by outside author)
- Article 5 (contributed by outside author)
- Article 6 (contributed by outside author)

Summary (written by you)

Book summary (written by you)

Back Matter:
- Appendix
- Glossary of terms
- Bibliographic references
- Resources / Links
- About the author
- Ordering information

Back Cover (with blurb)

Six of one, half-a-dozen of the other?

The number of articles you use in any section of the book is up to you. You can use the same number of articles in each section—or not.

How long is too long?

How long should an article (or section, or book) be? My favorite response is, "Writing is like a woman's skirt, it has to be long enough to cover the subject, but short enough to be interesting!"

Written and edited by...

Since you have written both the Introduction to the book and the Book summary, you are indeed one of the authors. You may also have added introductory and summary information for each section, as well as comments on each article.

Chances are you may need to edit some of the articles for content and possibly length. Include permission to edit the article in the release you have every author sign.

Are we there yet?

Depending on your determination and passion, you could produce at least two and possibly several more books per year using this idea.

What are you waiting for? Get Started!

Hire a ghostwriter

Some people have a talent for coming up with really good ideas. In fact, they can probably outline or storyboard the whole book, but by choice or by temperament they have no desire to actually write the book.

That is not a problem. You can hire a ghostwriter. Who do you think writes most of the books for celebrities and politicians?

Check with writing groups in your area for reputable ghostwriters.[12] You may be able to work out a plan where you come up with the ideas and outlines, the ghostwriter fleshes them out, and you both share the profits equally.

Hybrid authorship

Another unique way to produce a book is through hybrid authorship, where you use several of the ideas presented here to develop your book.

You may have a great idea and a strong opinion on a particular subject, but maybe not enough material to cover your subject.

So, you contact an expert on the subject and digitally record an interview, which you later transcribe.

In addition, you may have run across a few articles at an article directory that really match the tone of your book, so you contact the authors for permission to use their material in your book.

---

[12] See www.PublishingSuccessOnline.com for the eBook "Ghostwriting"

Do whatever works

The pride of ownership may be a motivating force that makes you want to write the whole book by yourself, but don't forego the possibility of writing books in collaboration with others.

Show me the money!

Rarely, does a single book make you enough money to retire or even just relax. Having several different books is the key to continuous streams of revenue. The more product (books) you have, the healthier your bank account.

Public domain

I am not a big fan of using documents that are in the public domain, especially if you are simply copying the work and putting your name on it as though you had written it.

I can see using elements of public domain materials to illustrate a point, or add more depth to your book, but I also think the original author should get full credit for that material—even if it is the U.S. Government.

Strike while the iron is hot!

In my humble opinion, the very best way to write a book is when you are consumed with passion about a particular topic and you have something to say to the rest of the world.

When you write with passion, your voice comes through, you sound authentic, and you provide unique solutions that benefit your readers.

The best time to write?

Now.

Writing is not typing your thoughts into the keyboard–that is recording.

Writing happens both consciously and unconsciously, as you go about your daily activities.

Thoughts and ideas will continue to simmer in the back of your mind until your passion or preparation bring the whole concept to a boiling point and you are ready to record it on a legal pad, a typewriter, a computer, or a digital recorder.

That first burst of creation, where the possibilities and potentials are endless, is the most exciting for me as a writer.

You are already a writer

Once you've got the idea for a book, you will find that a unique mechanism in your brain called the reticular activating system will start searching for anything and everything related to the topic of your book.

It's not synchronicity or serendipity; it's a new level of focus.

You will simply start noticing elements you need for your book.

Make sure you always carry a pen, index cards, a piece of paper or a digital recorder to capture these unique ideas as they reveal themselves to you.

I know a woman who got ideas while driving. Because she could not pull over or take her focus off the road to write a note, she would call her home answering machine and record her thoughts and ideas on voice mail.[13]

Every night she went home and transcribed her notes, one at a time, on a carbon message form, so she could tear off the top message to create her storyboards and still have a carbon of all her thoughts and ideas.

She literally wrote a book while driving.

You can make an excuse or you can make an effort!

You have been presented with several techniques to write, produce, or develop a book on any topic you desire.

So what are you going to do?

"Someday I'll" never comes

Too many people live on the fantasy island of Someday Isle. People who live on this island are forever declaring, "Someday, I'll do this...," "Someday, I'll do that..." There is no "someday," there is only today.

The only thing I can guarantee you is that as you grow older, the days begin slipping by faster and faster.

Will you accomplish something today or will you make an excuse?

---

[13] From a safety standpoint, it would be best to pull over and make the call to your home answering service. Anything that takes your attention off the road could lead to an accident.

If you think you can, you can!

I believe you can write a book.

You can start right now.

Pick your topic, preferably something you are passionate about.

Start collecting your thoughts and ideas, then go back to the beginning of this book and fill out your first storyboard.

Once you have your plan, use one of (or many of) the ideas in this book to write, produce, and develop your book.

Ready, Fire, Aim!

You will never know whether you hit the bull's eye with your writing unless you take a shot.

Writing a book is similar to target shooting; you must take a shot (write some text) and see whether you hit the target (got your point across).

Once you see where your first shot landed, you can adjust your sights and improve your score in both target shooting and in writing a book.

Good luck!

I look forward to seeing your new book online and in the bookstores.

Part 6: Editing: Easy Steps to Improve Your Writing

Is it better like this, or like this?

Good writing deserves at least two sets of eyeballs: yours and your editor's.

Many writers are "one-draft wonders" who publish the first thoughts that pop into their minds.

Abbreviated text in e-mail and Twitter-type messages seem to have significantly lowered the bar in communications.

Your product or business is communication by text, regardless of format. Please consider employing a few of the editing methods listed below, if not an actual editor, especially if you have a book-length manuscript.

However, to get your money's worth out of an editor, send as clean a manuscript as possible. Below are a few hints you can use to make your writing look its best.

1. Rest before reviewing.

   Take some time off, preferably 48 hours to a week, and do something else while the ink on your newly minted manuscript dries. After a rest, you'll return with a new perspective to edit your piece for clarity, competence, and compelling communication.

2. Five-sense your writing.

   Bring your story alive by going through it at least five times, once for each sense.

   The five senses are seeing, hearing, smelling, touching, and tasting.

On the first pass, look for ways to communicate the sense of sight and imagery by adding descriptions of color, lightness and darkness, speed of motion, or anything the reader would "see" in your writing.

Add specific elements to the piece for each of the other senses until you create an experience for a reader that literally enables them to feel they are in the book or article experiencing it firsthand.

And yes, even non-fiction writers can use this technique to make a book more interesting.

3. Decimate Your Writing.

   Decimate means to eliminate one word out of every 10 in your manuscript.

   For example, words like "and, or, but, nor, so, and that" and almost all words ending in "-ly" (adverbs) can be eliminated. Obviously, this is not true all the time, but it is true enough of the time to significantly tighten your writing.

   (Was "obviously" really necessary at the beginning of the last sentence?)

   Avoid weak openings (i.e. *generally, it is, there is, usually,* **or** *if*). The above example would be much stronger if I deleted the beginning word (*Obviously*).

4. Remove excess "its."

   While the Addams Family may be overjoyed when Cousin It shows up for a visit, too many "its" in your manuscript can lead to confusion. Eliminate excess "its." Use the name or noun instead.

You can also delete words like "thing" and "stuff."[14]

5. Exterminate he's and she's and him's and her's (also: they, them, one).

    Just like the word "it", over use of he, she, him and her can also be confusing.

    Exterminate at least one third of the he's and she's and him's and her's you find lurking in your manuscript and replace them with the proper name of the person.

    Or, rewrite the sentence so it is not only grammatically correct, but stronger!

    Instead of "He climbed the hill after her." Try, "Jack raced up the hill after the girl of his dreams, toting that damned pail of water every painful step."

    Overuse of pronouns is a lazy way to write and with some work on your word choices, you create a GREAT sentence instead.

    Also, a convention, not adopted by all grammarians and editors, is the singular "they" to eliminate the repetition of the awkward he/she in an effort to be politically correct.

    Go with the singular "they" to make the reading experience smoother and tick off Grammosauruses, oops, I mean old English teachers.

---

[14] I remember It and Thing from *The Addam's Family*, but I don't remember Stuff.

6. Active verbs rule!

   Use the "Find" command on your word processor toolbar to search for the verbs "is" and "was" in your manuscript, and then replace as many as you can with action-oriented verbs.

7. Passive voice is boring.

   Again, action-oriented verbs are more powerful than most verbs ending with "ing." Use the "Find" command on your toolbar to search for verbs ending with "ing" and replace them with more action or active verbs.

8. In most cases, prepositional phrases clutter and confuse, in writing articles about anything.

   The simple and direct words, "Prepositional phrases clutter and confuse" describe this tip much better than the version above it cluttered with prepositional phrases.

   Eliminate unnecessary prepositional phrases.

9. Read your writing aloud.

   When you edit by reading your writing aloud, you will be amazed at all the mistakes and awkward phrasing you'll find. Missing elements you thought about in your head but never wrote on the page will also reveal themselves.

   In addition, natural pauses (moments when you take a breath) may indicate good places to put a comma.

   Reading out loud may also indicate where paragraphs should naturally begin and end.

Read to an audience of one or two people (when possible) to get feedback on the content and clarity of your message.

10. Review from back to front.

The mind tends to fill in what it thinks should be on the written page and, after reading your manuscript several times, even text that is clearly in error may still seem acceptable.

You can overcome this obstacle to proofing (and spell checking) by starting from the end of your article and reading backwards, from right to left and from bottom to top.

Using this method, you will catch many spelling errors your computer misses, because even though the words are spelled correctly, they may be incorrect for the sentence.

11. Find a starving college senior majoring in English.

Probably the best method for great editing is to find a starving college senior with a major in English and pay this student one dollar for every mistake found in the manuscript.

You can be sure the manuscript will be closely scrutinized by the student editor who has probably survived on Ramen noodles and PB&J sandwiches for the past four to six years and is looking forward to a real meal.

Besides, they can add the project to a work portfolio or resume' when they look for a "real" job.

12. For more conversational sounding speech it's better to use contractions.

    "I can't" vs. "I cannot"

13. Vary the rhythm and pacing of your sentences.
    (No more than 10 - 15 words per sentence.)

14. Be specific rather than general in your writing.

    Example: Many people attended... (vague)
    85 people attended ...   (specific)

15. Any action you want your reader or audience to take should be easy to accomplish with no difficult steps or tedious directions to follow. Tell the reader exactly what to do. People will not take the time to figure things out. Lead them by the hand.

16. Break up long and boring articles by using a question and answer format.

17. Each word used should be short, familiar, and the meaning clear. Don't try to impress the reader with your consummate vocabulary. Eliminate unnecessary words. Short and simple words are best. Use language the common person can understand.

18. Use information or statistics that are personal and down to earth for the audience.

19. Perk up your writing with:
    • startling facts
    • intriguing questions
    • the debunking of a common myth or rumor
    • a funny or poignant anecdote
    • breaking information and,

- a slice of life or interesting comparison piece of information.

20. Be sure to include both opening and closing quotation marks where applicable.

21. Keep an eye on your verb tense. It's easy to slip from singular to plural, even within a single sentence.

22. Keep the same "point of view" throughout the piece. Sometimes you start off writing from the "I think..." perspective and end up saying "we should..." by the end of the document.

23. Check for accurate punctuation. The exclamation mark is often overused!!! Isn't the question mark often forgotten.[15]

24. *Use an easy-to-read typeface .*

Editing is not an exact science

Technology and culture are making significant changes in what we accept in written form, causing many "old school" editors to throw up their hands in despair. Even so, as a writer, you should keep in mind that you represent yourself initially with a book, an email, a web site, a brochure, or a letter. How you come across in writing can make a significant difference in publishing and selling your book (and in landing a contract or speaking gig).

---

[15] No, I didn't forget the question mark. I was illustrating a point. Besides, most people need to find mistakes to feel superior. (You can now imagine me on my knees) "I'm not worthy, I'm not worthy!"

Proofread your documents

First impressions still count. You don't want to send out or publish documents with spelling errors. Even worse, send out documents with critical information that is incorrect.

The solution is to proofread, spell check, and proofread again.

When you are done proofing the document, get someone else to proof it for you.

I constantly write and rewrite articles, but after a while the words begin to sound correct because I am used to seeing and mentally hearing them in that order. When that happens, I usually leave the document alone for a few days and then come back to it with a fresh perspective.

I find that asking someone else to read and proof the document invariably turns up several mistakes I can't believe I let slip by.

Accurate information

Make sure all the information in your document is accurate. Check the following carefully:

- information placed in quotes
- days
- dates
- times
- addresses
- name spellings
- prices
- phone numbers and,
- make sure names in photograph captions (and quotations) are spelled correctly and placed in the proper order.

Spelling & grammar-checking software

Most computers have programs that can help you; however, you still need to check up on your computer.

The spell checker in your computer won't know the difference between the words: *"their," "there,"* and *"they're."*

Make sure you are using the right word. In addition, if a word is spelled incorrectly, but is still recognized as a word, the computer will not catch it.

> **Example:** *"For more information... "*
> *"Foe more information... "*

"Foe," meaning enemy, is a perfectly acceptable word as far as the computer is concerned, however, if you don't want your reader to become a foe, proofread your work carefully.

Juan and his burro (a short story)

Perhaps the following story will help summarize the need for proofreading every document before you offer it for sale to the paying public.

I have an author friend named Juan, who moved to the United States from South America.

Upon arriving in the U.S., Juan learned to speak, read, and write the English language.

Feeling proficient in his communications, Juan decided to open a proofreading business.

In one of his business brochures, Juan wrote a brief biography of his life. In particular, he told of how every day in South

America he would ride his burro from the village to the big-city where his business was located.

Unfortunately, Juan was confused over how to spell the word *"burro."* Remembering that the English word *"window"* had a silent "w" at the end, Juan spelled the name for his riding animal as *"b-u-r-r-o-w."*

As we all know, a *"burro"* is a small donkey or mule, and a *"burrow" spelled with a "w"* is a hole in the ground where small creatures live.

Naturally, I couldn't resist saying to Juan: *"If you can't tell the difference between your ass and a hole in the ground, you shouldn't be a proofreader!"*

Who are you writing for?

I think this is an important question to ask in this section on editing, because you will be editing your book for a particular audience.

Not everybody will buy your book!

Have a good cry. Blow your nose. Now, sit up straight and pay attention.

Focus on a niche

Contrary to popular opinion, a niche is not the Grinch's pocket-sized pet with only one hair growing out of the top of its head. A niche is a select group of people with interests similar to yours, who will be interested in your topic and your style of writing.

If your niche (group of interested consumers with open wallets) is only 1 percent of 100,000 people, that's 1000 people. If you sell your book to 1000 people for $10 a book, you just made $10,000.00.

Call me crazy, but I'll take $10K to the bank any day. I don't give a rat's rump what the other 99,000 people think of my book.

If you tell two friends, then they tell two friends…

Once you find a group of people who like what and how you write, you've got a market for future books.

The best advertising in the world is **_word of mouth_**. People who like what you write will tell other people of similar interest about your book and your fame and fortune will soon grow exponentially.

Product is king

If you really are interested in making good money, product, or in this case, content is king. Keep developing additional content using the same voice, personality, and writing style that got you here in the first place.

Be who you are

Let the "real you" escape through your fingertips onto the page. If you have a snarky sense of humor, let it flow. Let your personality show in your writing and don't even attempt to please anybody but yourself.

Part 7:

Book Titles: Key to Sales Success

Book Titles: Key to Sales Success

Your book title is a critical element in the success of your book. Okay, that should seem rather obvious to most of you, but I have often been mystified at the titles I have seen on what could have been successful books.

Sometimes a book title is decided by the author's ego–almost always a bad idea, but many times the title choice is simply the first idea the author came up with and then decided to write the book around the title.

Your original idea, or working title while writing your grand opus, is a great starting point, but keep in mind there may be a second right idea, a third, a fourth, maybe even a hundred right ideas.

Once you have explored at least that many ideas for a title you can narrow the choices based on the market or a "niche" segment of that market you feel most needs what you have to say.

How are you going to stand out in the crowd?

According to Jim Milliot in *Publishers Weekly* (4/14/2010) the total book output (published) rose 87 percent last year to over one million books.

Word of mouth is still king in advertising

People will most often hear about your title before ever seeing your book, so the title must be clear and to the point.

A book title is really a headline or the keywords in an online search, and many times a subject line in an email. If your topic is clear and the keywords are front-loaded in the title, your book has a better chance of being found by search engines and the people.

My theory

Headlines hook them.

Content keeps them.

Value sells them a product.

Your title, headline, subject line, or blog post header must attract the viewer's interest before the other million search results do.

In an Internet world...

Keywords are the words and phrases people use to search for your topic on a search engine like Google.

Always put the primary keyword at the beginning of your title, headline, or subject line.

For instance...

I wrote a book titled *Back Handsprings: The Secret Techniques.*

Originally, the title was going to be *Secret Techniques to Learn Back Handsprings.*

Then I realized the book would always be listed under "*Secret Techniques...*" first in *Books in Print* and anywhere else.

I had to change the title so the two most important keywords, "*Back Handsprings...*" were front-loaded in the title.

Does the title of your book have the most important keywords at the beginning?

What are my keywords?

Post a chapter of your book as an html page on your website then do a density check at: http://webconfs.com/keyword-density-checker.php to determine key words for your title (keyword strings).

You can also check out the keywords your competitors use by going to their websites and clicking *Source* on the menu bar, then click on *View* and you will be able to see the html coding for the page. Look for keywords in the coding and you can get a list of keywords used.

You can also go to online booksellers like Amazon.com and review the tags listed for each book.

Titling your book

- Present only one idea or key element in your title.

- A title of seven words or less is a good rule of thumb.

- Use a subtitle to clarify the main title.

- Keep it simple and direct. Remember, specific titles are better than vague ones. Use the KISSU method: Keep It Short, Simple, and Understandable.

- Remember always, your reader is asking the question, *"What's in this book that will help me?"* Can you answer that question with your book's title?

Advice from the master

In **The Copywriter's Handbook,** copywriter extraordinaire Bob Bly[16] sets forth eight time-tested headline categories that compel action and rake in sales.

Note: Where Bob has written the word "*headline*" you can mentally substitute the word "*title.*"

- *Direct Headlines* go straight to the heart of the matter, without any attempt at cleverness. Bly gives the example of **Pure Silk Blouses – 30 Percent Off** as a headline that states the selling proposition directly. A direct blog post title might read **Free SEO E-book**.

- An *Indirect Headline* takes a more subtle approach. It uses curiosity to raise a question in the reader's mind, which the body copy answers. Often a double meaning is utilized, which is useful online. An article might have the headline **Fresh Bait Works Best** and yet have nothing to do with fishing, because it's actually about writing timely content that acts as **link bait**.

- A *News Headline* is pretty self-explanatory, as long as the news itself is actually, well... news. A product announcement, an improved version, or even a content

---

[16] http://tinyurl.com/3c8dyee

scoop can be the basis of a compelling news headline. Think **Introducing Flickr 2.0** or **My Exclusive Interview With Steve Jobs**.

- The *How to Headline* is everywhere, online and off, for one reason only – it works like a charm. Bly says that "Many advertising writers claim if you begin with the words *how to*, you can't write a bad headline." An example would be, umm… oh yes… the title of this post.

- Another effective technique is called the *Reason Why Headline*. Your body text consists of a numbered list of product features or tips, which you then incorporate into the headline, such as **Two Hundred Reasons Why Open Source Software Beats Microsoft**. It's not even necessary to include the words "reasons why." This technique is actually the underlying strategy behind the ubiquitous blogger "list" posts, such as **8 Ways to Build Blog Traffic**.

- Finally, we have the *Testimonial Headline*, which is highly effective because it presents outside proof that you offer great value. This entails taking what someone else has said about you, your product or service, and using their actual words in your headline. Quotation marks let the reader know that they are reading a testimonial, which will continue in the body copy. An example might be **"I Read Copyblogger First Thing Each Morning," admits Angelina Jolie**.

- A *Question Headline* must do more than simply ask a question, it must be a question that, according to Bly, the reader can empathize with or would like to see answered. He gives this example from *Psychology Today*: **Do You Close the Bathroom Door Even When You're the Only One Home?** Another example used *way too much* in Internet marketing guru-ville is **Who Else Wants to Get Rich Online?**

- The *Command Headline* boldly tells the prospect what he needs to do, such as Exxon's old **Put a Tiger in Your Tank** campaign. Bly indicates that the first word should be a strong verb demanding action, such as **Subscribe to Copyblogger Today!**

Test, test, test

Send your book cover and title concepts out to at least one thousand of your best friends, family, and relatives (by email) to see what kind of feedback you get. If one title or book cover dominates in the selection process, you likely have a winner.

"It is with words as with sunbeams. The more they are condensed, the deeper they burn."

- Robert Southey

"A sentence should contain no unnecessary words, a paragraph no unnecessary sentences, for the same reason that a drawing should have no unnecessary lines and a machine no unnecessary parts. "

- William Strunk, Jr.
The Elements of Style, 1918

Part 8:

Tracking Your Book's Development

Document guidelines

I used to have the world's worst filing system, now I know at least six other people are in worse shape, but I think a few basic guidelines will help you to keep track of your documents.

Document layout

The layout of each document should be in standard manuscript style:

- The document should have a minimum margin of one inch all around.

- Double-space the entire document.[17]

- Use a standard font such as Times New Roman or Arial 12 point.

- Create a header with the document name, copyright date, and author name.

- Create a footer with the page number.

- Indents on the first line of a paragraph are optional.

- Set a 12 point space between each paragraph, not a hard carriage return.

---

[17] Use double-spacing when you are still working on your drafts, sending it out for edits, or submitting to an agent or publisher. You will change the spacing to single when you paginate or lay out your book.

- Use standard punctuation and grammar throughout.

- Proof all documents for spelling and grammar errors before transmission.

Document naming guidelines

- Use only lower case letters

- Use an underscore between words

- Include the document title, author name, and date

For example: An article titled "Scene Sketch" would have a document title:

scene_sketch_rikfeeney_092611.doc

Any time you make even the smallest change to a document, save it with that day's date, then add an a, b, or c after it to note a different version.

Any other document-naming scheme may cause files to be lost or displaced.

Folders

Use the document naming guidelines to title the folders within which you keep your written documents. If you are using software to make copies of your documents off site (like Carbonite) you will likely want to keep your files under the

"Documents" or "My Documents" directory to make sure they are constantly backed up.

The blue screen of death

Have you ever been working on your computer and suddenly the screen blanks out and you find yourself staring at the blue screen of death?

For whatever reason, a virus, a fried motherboard, or a power surge and suddenly everything you wrote that day is gone; maybe even the whole book is gone if your hard drive gets zapped.

Back up! Back up! Back up!

There are several ways you can back up your book and make sure you always have access to at least the information written within the past day.

Auto save

Many word processors have an "auto save" function that saves a document at predetermined times. Set your auto save function to make a copy of your document every five or 10 minutes.

Ctrl-S

Besides the auto save function, you can always press the "Ctrl" button and the "S" button at the same time to save your work.

Make it a habit to frequently hit "Ctrl-S" and save your work. If something is burning on the stove, the UPS man is at the front door, or the baby is crying, always hit "Ctrl-S" before you get up to put out the fire.

I guarantee you; cats know you have been pouring your heart out in a one-time epiphany of literary genius. As soon as you are out of sight, they will jump up on the keyboard and try to stomp out your efforts by dancing all over the keyboard.

The "save" icon

You can also do a quick click of your mouse at the "save" icon on the toolbar at the top of your document.

Print a hard copy

When you are done writing for the day, always print out a hard copy and save it in a three-ring binder.

3-ring binder

Get yourself a three-ring binder with hard or soft sides that come with plastic "preview panes" on the front and back covers.

Dividers

Get yourself a couple packages of dividers to separate front matter from chapters, and Supporting Points from introductions and summaries, and the meat of the book from the back matter.

I think it is easier to flip between the pages and sections of a hard copy inside a three-ring notebook than using electronic files.

You can mark it up easier with Post-its, highlighters, and the ubiquitous red pen.

Portable storyboard (paper)

Create a simple paper version of your storyboard by opening a word document in Landscape orientation, then add a table with five rows and 10 columns. Expand the table to cover the printable area of the paper and you have a basic storyboard template.[18]

Add chapter titles and supporting idea notes using your word processor, then print them out and add them to the front of your 3-ring binder, so you can track which Supporting Points you have written and which still need work.

Portable storyboard (plastic sleeves)

You can also go to your local office supply store and buy plastic sheets for holding business cards.

Each sheet normally holds 10 cards in two columns of five cards each. With three plastic business card sheets, you could outline up to a 12-chapter book by placing chapter titles across the top of each plastic sleeve. The four empty sleeves under each chapter title would be filled with your Supporting Points.

---

[18] The size of the storyboard is up to you. 5X4, 5X8, or 5 rows X 10 columns?

You can also use the backs of old business cards, buy blank business cards from a printer, or purchase business card blanks made for printing on inkjet and laser printers. Done this way, you can type your information on each card using your word processor, then print out your storyboard.

Front and back cover drafts

Another cool thing to do is make mock-ups of the front and back covers of your book and slip them into the preview panes on the front and back of the 3-ring binder.

Using Microsoft Publisher® or the current version of Adobe Photoshop Elements®, you can create the first draft of your book cover using clipart or photographs from stock photography sites.[19]

Seeing your book cover makes the final publication seem all the more real.

Note: Do not use photographs in your book or on the book cover without permission. Many stock photo sites sell "royalty free" licenses for a very modest fee.

A sense of satisfaction

I get a tremendous sense of satisfaction as I see the notebook fill with my writing, and so will you. At the same time, you will be creating a hard copy of your book to work from, should your computer decide to die unexpectedly.

---

[19] See Resources for stock photography sites.

Jump drive

Jump drive, flash drive, and USB drive are all names for those funky little rectangular devices that plug in to the USB port of your computer. Jump drives are external memory devices that allow you to save information and even transport it between computers like your laptop and your desktop.

Jump drives come in many sizes like 2GB, 4GB, 8GB and more, with the price of the drive normally escalating along with the amount of memory.

A 2GB drive is often adequate to copy all files relating to your book unless you have quite a few pictures. Picture files can be memory hogs, so if you have a lot of photographs or illustrations, you may want to get an 8GB jump drive.

Simply plug your memory drive into a USB port, then go to the "File" menu on your word processor and click on "Save As." I normally save my files as MS Word 97-2003 files with the ".doc" extension. When I do this, I can click on "Computer" and choose my jump drive, which will likely be titled Drive F or Drive G depending on your computer, then I click "Save."

Warning: Before removing your jump drive, make sure you right click on the icon for the drive (under "Computer") and select "Safely Remove." Wait until the computer tells you it is safe to remove the jump drive or you could fry it and lose all your information as well as the jump drive.

Email back up

A simple way to back up your writing is to email it to yourself. Simply copy the document and paste it into an email that you address to yourself.

Put the document name in the subject line.

You can access your files from virtually any computer this way.

Carbonite

I have lost computers and files several times in the past. Once, I accidentally overwrote a whole book manuscript with another file.

Fortunately, I had a hard copy of the book and was able to send it to a transcriptionist to get the file keyed in to a Word document again.

Now, I invest in a service called Carbonite.[20] Carbonite continuously backs up the data on my hard drive to an offsite server.

If I come home and find my abode has been washed away in a Biblical flood or has gone up in flames like Sodom and Gomorrah,[21] I can always contact Carbonite and have the files restored to my new computer.

(Oh boy! I'm getting a new computer.)

---

[20] There are other companies that provide similar services.
[21] God has tried to get me on more than one occasion.

"The muscles of writing are not so visible, but they are just as powerful: determination, attention, curiosity, a passionate heart."

- Natalie Goldberg

The Grand Finale

Happy trails to you...

You and I have covered a lot of territory in these few short pages, and if you have made it this far, I am willing to bet you will soon have a book published.

Great ideas

You are a wealth of knowledge. Scour your personal experiences, your favorite hobbies, your various jobs, or your personal interests, and you will undoubtedly find unique thoughts, ideas, and talents that can benefit other people.

A nonfiction book is simply a prepackaged solution to someone else's problem.

Pull your knowledge together into a book, a short report, or an article, and help relieve someone else's pain.

Make an effort or make an excuse

You have all the tools you need with the Top-10 Writing System Outline. You also have several alternate ways to produce a book. So you can make an effort and write the book for potential fun, fame, and fortune, or you can make an excuse and watch life pass you by. (If you choose the latter, imagine me making the world's smallest violin with my fingers and playing "My Heart Bleeds for You.")

I know. You want to smack me, but you can't reach me, can you? Nyah, nyah...

Every winner was once a beginner!

You are allowed to make mistakes. Remember, good judgment comes from experience and experience often comes from bad judgment.

So go ahead and start writing. When you're done, present it at a critique group or hire an editor. Keep polishing and rewriting your piece until you are ready to publish.

...until we meet again!

When you are ready to publish,[22] you can experiment digitally by publishing with the Amazon Kindle or the Barnes & Noble Nook and who knows, you just might become the next Amanda Hocking or John Locke!

"My works are like water, the works of
the great masters are like wine;
but everyone drinks water."

- Mark Twain

---

[22] See www.PublishingSuccessOnline.com for my next book, "Publishing for Penny-Pinchers!"

<u>Appendix A:</u>

Are

You

Still

Here?

Great Ideas: Where do they come from?

One summer day Knowledge invited Inspiration to a picnic and a new idea was the result of the flirtation between the two. In fact, many new ideas were also born that day when Experience and Desire got together, and who could forget the ruckus Need made chasing Fantasy all over the place? In short, this was the beginning of all Creativity, even though today you might think creativity has almost vanished from the world.

Believe and achieve

Today, the problem regarding creativity and the birth of new ideas is a belief in self, rather than the belief in personal creative ability. To quote Valerie Parv in her book *The Idea Factory*, "to be creative, you must believe you are creative."

Break out of your rut

There are many reasons why we aren't as creative as we could be. Roger von Oech relates one reason in his book *A Whack On The Side Of the Head*. von Oech thinks that most people have gotten used to routines and habits and have forgotten how to think new and creative thoughts.

While routines and habits are great for keeping order in society (i.e. people stop at red lights), routine thinking is not good enough for solving the new and different problems that surface as we continue to grow.

Skip school?

Another reason we may not be as creative is that our schools and educational systems stop or greatly reduce activities that would develop the right hemisphere, the side of the brain associated in most people with creative, abstract thought.

In her book, *Drawing on the Right Side of the Brain*, Betty Edwards theorizes that most creative education in school stops somewhere in the elementary years.

I think that Edwards and von Oech are right, but I also think that people in general are way more creative than they realize. Many times personal need combined with desire or fantasy can cause an individual to be creative.

Rounding first base...

Have you ever seen a boy on a date with a good-looking girl? Creative desire is definitely in high gear as he plans and plots his way through the date. (Maybe testosterone should be renamed creativity.) No matter how many times the good-looking girl shuts him down, this boy keeps coming up with creative ways to make it around the bases and get home.

Young at heart

Another good way to get a lesson in creativity is to watch young children. They have few if any preconceived notions about what an object is or how something should work, so they simply make up concepts and rules as they play.

I've seen youngsters eating ice cream with a fork. Perhaps that's a good idea for someone watching their weight; they would only eat half as much in each bite.

Young children easily keep themselves amused for hours on end because they come at every activity with a certain wonder or beginner's mind. Doesn't it just blow you away when you spend a fortune on a gift, and the child spends the next three hours playing with the wrapping?

Become a child again

One way you can develop your creative abilities (like a child) and generate new ideas is by keeping your mind open to the wonder and possibilities all around you. Silence the voice in your mind that wants to criticize new ideas or even edit them before you have had a chance to apply them. I believe everyone has a creative bone that still works within him or her, especially as it relates to an area of personal interest, passion, or skill (like writing a book).

Aspects of creative individuals:

- The creative individual anticipates new trends and/or events.

- You are creative when you develop new ways of doing things.

- When you inspire others to be innovative and use their own brand of genius, you are being creative.

- If you are dissatisfied with the status quo and seek new solutions, you are being creative.

- Creativity is applying skills, techniques, or ideas from other disciplines to the problem at hand.

- Being naive is a great way to be creative. With no preconceptions, you can come up with ideas others may neglect.

- Focusing your thoughts and talents in one area can help you create.

- Keeping alive your ability to wonder, question, and admire the whole of creation.

- Sharing your ideas with others is a great way to gain additional insights.

- Absorbing various stimuli without editing for meaning like books, TV, movies, the newspaper, watching people at the mall, a bug trying to get outside, a cat chasing a mouse, all teach you creativity.

- Have an adventure. Go white-water rafting, jump out of a plane (with a parachute), or maybe even write a book!

- Relax, something most people do far too seldom. Just allow that stream of consciousness to flow through your head and see what ideas pop up. This can best be accomplished watching the fire in the fireplace, watching the waves crash on the beach, or just enjoying a sunset.

- Be inquisitive. Like a young child always ask why, and when given an answer keep asking why at least five times or until you are smacked!

- Change your habits. Go to work a new way. Eat something new. If you workout at night, move your workout to the morning. Break out of your daily rut. Some people say a rut is but a shallow grave.

- Learn something new, something that has nothing to do with your current job or interests.

- Read a book from a different genre than you normally read. If you like romance, try reading fantasy. If you read science fiction, try reading a biography.

- Learn to speak a new language.

- Take a trip to somewhere you have never been.

- Take some time for reflection and meditation. It could be religious prayer or simply contemplating your belly button.

- Hitchhike on other people's ideas and make them your own by adding your thoughts and creativity. As Thomas Edison once said: "Your idea has to be original only in its adaptation to your current problem or project."

- Play "what if?" What if you had to work from midnight to seven in the morning? What would happen if starving artists made their paintings out of edible materials? What if all the criminals locked up had to earn their keep? What would they do? What if women were only allotted 2000 words a day? Would we need psychiatrists anymore?

- Five-sense your ideas. How would your idea be different using the sense of smell, taste, sight, touch, or hearing?

- As Napoleon Hill describes in his book *Laws of Success,* create a "Master Mind" with three to five people from other disciplines. When the group gets together and begins coming up with ideas, it seems to create a sixth or "Master Mind" that is unique from its individual parts. What kind of ideas would you create with your Master Mind?

- Free write or do "stream of consciousness" writing. For 10 minutes just sit down and write anything that pops in to your head.

"A great nonfiction book is a prepackaged (creative) solution to somebody else's pain or problem."

You now know several ways to be more creative as an individual. As I have stated earlier in this book, all is for naught if you do not have some way of recording these little gems of creativity.

Capturing creativity

Take notes everywhere you go. Carry an index card and a pen with you at all times to jot down those great ideas that pop into your head when you least expect them. Great ideas always have a way of coming to you when you least expect them. I believe it happens when the mind is not intensely focused on some project or activity, when the subconscious can slip through with a new idea or answer to a problem you have posed previously.

Only if I have to pee...

I hate getting up in the middle of the night, so I keep a digital recorder beside my bed. I also keep one in my car so I can dictate my thoughts wherever I happen to be driving.

But, no matter what, I always carry an index card or piece of paper and a pen with me to capture the "aha!" of a new idea. Later, I transcribe these ideas into a computer file for ease in research or retrieving my ideas. I can also lay the index cards out in rows on the table. Each row from top to bottom includes topics from similar areas. When I am done, I usually have the chapters of a new book laid out and ready to go. (Just like the Top-10 Writing System you learned earlier.)

Still stuck?

Some days writing is about as much fun as eating a cupcake covered with mustard icing. It's just not something you want to do. But, because the world is patiently waiting for the awesome book inside your head, I present you with a technique known as "SCAMPER" (author unknown), which uses a series of questions to help focus your topic and presents you with new ways of thinking about it.

Each of the letters in SCAMPER stands for a unique way of being creative with any project or idea.

> **S**-What can you **substitute**?

> **C**-What can you **combine**?

> **A**-What can you **adapt**?

> **M**-What can you **magnify, miniaturize**, or **multiply**?

> **P**-What can you **put to other uses**?

> **E-What else, who else, where else** (applied to each of the ways listed)

> **R**-What can you **rearrange** or **reverse**?

Apply the SCAMPER questions to any of your chapter titles, Supporting Points or writing in general you want to change or improve, or use it just to be creative.

"-est Technique"

Another technique I use to come up with new and creative ideas is the "-est" technique. Think of all the adjectives that you can add "-est" to that relate to the topic or subject you want to write about. It is sure to give you some great ideas. You could even keep a list close to where you write of your favorite adjectives like:

- biggest

- ugliest

- fastest

- youngest

- drunkest

- sloppiest

- prettiest or

- oldest.

Can't see the forest for the trees

Even using the techniques already described, it is still possible to get stuck in one frame of mind while searching for ideas to make your writing new and creative. What you need is something to kick you out of your normal pattern of problem solving or idea generation.

Using Tarot cards

Tarot cards are helpful in kicking me out of my normal thinking habits. The idea (as I understand it) is that you concentrate on one question or concern while shuffling the cards, like "Is my blind date a dog?" Then lay out 10 cards. Each card has a specific meaning relating to its placement.

For instance, the card in the #1 spot "shows the influence affecting the questioner; the atmosphere surrounding the matter in question." If I get the King of Cups in that spot, which says on it "Beware of ill-will," it's a sure bet I am not going on that date!

There are still nine other cards each with a meaning regarding its placement and message. By asking questions about what I am writing and getting random draws from the cards, I whack my thinking into other areas.

Every time I shuffle the cards, I come out with different combinations for the same question. It helps me to think of the writing problem from other points of view.

I don't even know what the cards are supposed to mean. I just go by the picture, by the title of the card, or the order in which they are arranged, which is usually more than enough to whack my thinking into other areas.

What head should I wear today?

Another technique I use is to put on someone else's head. In other words, I imagine that I am that person.

How would Batman handle this problem, or Mother Teresa, maybe even the Marquis de Sade? Once I put myself into their shoes or Bat-cape, depending on my need, I try to imagine how each would approach the situation creatively.

You are the problem

Sometimes I simply imagine that I am the problem or the idea. How would I solve my own situation? Taking on the attributes of the concept or idea is a great way to conquer idea block.

Legal disclaimer

After this total immersion approach to creativity and idea development for your writing, it is now time to trot out the suits with the appropriate warnings and disclaimers.

First, do not fall in love with the first idea or the first words you come up with. When searching for a solution to a problem, Roger von Oech advises that you not stop at the first "right answer," but that you search for a second, third, fourth, or maybe 100th right answer. The theory being the more options you generate the better the choice you will make.

According to French philosopher Emile Chartier, "*Nothing is more dangerous than an idea when it is the only one you have.*"

I'm so glad we had this time together...

You have learned all you need to know about combining knowledge and experience with need, desire, and fantasy and can now create your own family of new ideas to help you write your book and ease someone else's pain or provide a solution to a problem.

Go forth and multiply! (your ideas that is)

Arrivederci!

Bon Chance!

Vaya con dios!

Hasty bananas!

Crappy Dime!

Get out of here and write!

"Nothing in the world can take the place of Persistence. Talent will not; nothing is more common than unsuccessful men with talent.
Genius will not; unrewarded genius is almost a proverb.
Education will not; the world is full of educated derelicts.
Persistence and determination alone are omnipotent."

- Calvin Coolidge, 30th president of US (1872 - 1933)

<u>Appendix B:</u>

Publishing Options

The Best Way to Publish?

Let me start off by saying there is no one best way to publish, there is only the way that is best for you. For some, traditional publishing could be the key, for others it may be Print-On-Demand technology, and for those of you with an entrepreneurial bent, independent publishing could be a great choice.

There are also ways to be published for FREE digitally with the Kindle, the Nook, and other eReaders, with Adobe eBooks, and several other digital methods.

Hybrid or cooperative publishing, where the author shares in some of the expenses, but also has more input into the publishing process, is also becoming more popular for authors who want a quality product and a little more control.

Let's take a brief look at each method.

Traditional Publishing

In today's world, traditional publishing houses prefer to be contacted by agents. Many houses will simply send a standard form rejection letter and return the manuscript unread.

The key to traditional publishing for most people involves acquiring an agent by sending a query letter, capturing an agent's interest, submitting a manuscript and praying the agent will agree to represent you.

It may take up to a year just to get an agent and another year or so before a publishing house accepts the book for publication.

If you do land a traditional publishing contract, be warned that you could lose a great deal of control over the editorial process, content, book cover design, pricing, and possibly even the title.

A major publisher may also want a detailed marketing plan, as well as someone (meaning the author) who is willing to be the "front guy" and show up at book signings, appearances, etc.

A major book publisher will also attempt to take all rights associated with the book within the body of the contract.

Book advances are rare and your royalty will probably be no higher than 10 percent of which your agent will get 15 to 20 percent.

Your royalty is based on what is left over after the book is sold wholesale to bookstores (40 to 50 percent off), distributor costs (15 to 20 percent), and again your agent's cut (15 to 20 percent). If the book, for sake of argument sells retail for $10.00, your royalty after everybody else gets their share will likely be 10 percent of $2.00 or twenty cents per book.

You will need to sell a significant number of books to make this a financially viable choice.

Some of the advantages of traditional publishing are the big guys have strong distribution networks, and the cachet of being able to say you have been published traditionally still has a strong appeal.

Print-on-Demand

Please note that Print-On-Demand or POD is a technology that can be appropriately used or significantly abused.

The biggest problem with self-publishing, commonly associated with the technology of Print-On-Demand is that 99 percent of the authors (in my estimation) are simply not ready to publish, because they have not had the book professionally edited or designed, and the book cover looks as if it were made by a third grader.

In the POD publishing scenario, you do have more control over the look and feel of your book than with a traditional publisher.

You normally pay escalating fees, depending on how much you want the POD publisher to do for your book.

Fees can range from around $500 to several thousand dollars.

POD might be a good deal for an author who just wants to write a book and let someone else do the selling and fulfillment of the end product: the book (notice I did not say marketing of the book).

Another advantage is there is no need to purchase quantities of the book, as they can be printed, packed, and shipped as they are ordered.

Some POD companies have minimum-pricing guidelines for books depending on trim size, page count, and whether the interior is black and white, grayscale, or color.

Since POD's function in some ways as print brokers, they will attach their fee as intermediaries to the cost of printing the book.

For instance, a book that may cost $3.00 each to print may cost the author $8.00 apiece when the POD publisher adds its fee to the book.

This could lead to overpricing a book, because the author must still take into account discounts required by stores, online outlets, consignment venues, and possibly small press distributors.

You might be able to squeak a dollar or two in "royalties" or profits per book. Of course, this all depends on which POD you work with. Some are better; some are worse; some are up to no good.[23]

A big advantage of POD publishing is getting your book to market somewhat faster than traditional publishing, having a bit more control over the end product, and the ability to order in quantities from a single copy to thousands of books.

Be on the lookout for vanity presses masquerading as true POD publishers. You could pay a great deal of money for a whole lot of nothing. Do your homework and research each POD before signing with them and never, ever allow a POD to control your copyright on the book.

Independent Book Publisher

One way to publish the book yourself is to use a traditional printer.

---

[23] The only POD company I recommend is www.Booklocker.com.

You can send requests for quotes to printers for short or long-run book pricing. The higher the print run, the lower the cost per piece, although you do have to shell out a chunk of money up front to pay for the print run and the cost to store the books away from the elements (weather, children, dust, spiders–please God not spiders!).

You, the author, are responsible for layout and design of the final product and for supplying appropriate files to the printer.

Print services companies

You can also independently publish through "print services" companies which are the same companies that, in some cases, print the books for many POD publishers.[24]

From a marketing standpoint, independent publishing via print services companies and having your own ISBN number may be the ideal way to maximize the potential for future rights sales and the ability to play with different marketing techniques.

You have complete control over the design, editing, layout, marketing, promotion, sales, and fulfillment of the book. Best of all...

You get to keep 100 percent of the profits!

The drawback to independent publishing is you are responsible for the design, editing, layout, marketing, promotion, sales, and fulfillment of the book.

---

[24] Lightning Source is one of the major print services companies. It's used by several POD publishers and is owned by Ingram, one of the largest book wholesalers on the planet. Contact www.lightningsource.com for more information.

It can be quite time consuming, especially if this is your first time publishing a book, however, there are many talented writers, editors, and graphic designers hungry to make a name for themselves that you can hire without breaking the bank.[25]

Marketing = Key to Success

Perhaps, the most important aspect of independent publishing, actually any type of publishing, is who will focus on the continuous marketing of the book once it is published?

"Writing the book and publishing it is 5% of the process, continuous marketing and promotion is the other 95%."

Cooperative (hybrid) book publishing

Cooperative or hybrid is defined on a publisher-by-publisher basis although for the most part you can think of cooperative publishers as lean, mean traditional publishers that require a financial commitment from the author, but allow a wider range of input and can usually get your book to market faster, within six months to a year.

As the author, you will have a great deal more input on all aspects of the book production process with the cooperative publishing process.

---

[25] You can find many talented freelancers through sites like www.elance.com and www.guru.com.

Digital book publishing

Ain't technology great! When your book is finished and formatted, you can get it published the same day online. Within 24 to 72 hours, you will be amazing people with your wit, romancing them with your charm, terrifying them with your thoughts on horror, taking them on flights of fancy, or likely after reading this book, solving some pain or problem for which they will be eternally grateful.

Doesn't it just make you feel all warm and fuzzy to want to be an author?

Digital publishing is a great way to experiment free in the publishing world.

The basics of digital publishing are easy. Go online to a digital publisher's site, let's pick a popular one like Kindle (https://kdp.amazon.com/self-publishing/signin). Fill out basic information like name and address, social security number (so they can send you royalties) and other book-related information.

Then you will upload your marketing image (book cover) and the book content (usually a MS Word file), which Amazon will convert into a Kindle book file. You even get to see a mock-up of a Kindle with your book on it, so you can see how the electronic version of the book will look when published.

If it looks good, you simply accept and save the file.

Congratulations, you are now a published author!

Of course, this is a gross simplification of the process. There will always be some headaches and glitches to deal with, because nothing is ever that easy.

The good news is the KDP (Kindle Digital Publishing) program has all sorts of video tutorials and free downloads about publishing your book to the Kindle.

The other good news

There are a wide range of digital publishing venues. Unfortunately, they do not all adhere to a single format, so you may have to do some additional formatting of your files to upload to different digital publishers.

Digital publishing venues

Kindle - https://kdp.amazon.com/self-publishing/signin

The Nook -
http://pubit.barnesandnoble.com/pubit_app/bn?t=pi_reg_home

Google - http://books.google.com/googlebooks/tour/

Adobe eBooks -
http://www.adobe.com/digitalpublishing/ebook/

Smashwords -
http://www.smashwords.com/about/how_to_publish_on_smashwords

You Publish - http://www.youpublish.com/

Scribd - http://www.scribd.com/

Time equals money

In my book, time equals money. **Traditional publishing** can be a three or four year process before your book finally makes it to the bookstores. That is time lost, and potentially significant amounts of money lost. How long will you experiment with this method?

Many **POD technology companies** have upfront costs and some effective price gouging techniques that can make this a rough ride. There are some quality POD companies that could fit your needs,[26] but do your homework and check each one out carefully.[27]

Independent publishing has a steep learning curve and requires a unique set of skills to make it work. The good news is that you can outsource many of the more cumbersome or difficult jobs to hungry freelancers ready and willing to work at a decent rate.

Cooperative or hybrid publishing can be a good choice for many writers when you feel an affinity with the publisher and can verify previously published works by this publisher of a quality acceptable to you.

Digital publishing in many cases is free, but has a significant learning curve to overcome to make sure your books are converted correctly and displayed on the eReader in a professional manner. You also need a professional marketing image (cover) and as with all publishing methods, you must still market the book consistently if you want to see sufficient sales to afford cheese on your macaroni.

---

[26] Try www.Booklocker.com.
[27] Get a copy of *The Fine Print of Self-Publishing*, Fourth Edition - Everything You Need to Know About the Costs, Contracts, and Process of Self-Publishing by Mark Levine.

What method of publishing is best for you?

There is no one best method.

There is only the method that is right for you.

Before deciding on how to publish your masterpiece, go online and search out the different methods, attend writer's groups and talk to other authors about their experiences with different methods of publishing, and definitely attend writer's conferences in your area and chat with agents, publishers, and other authors about the publishing experience.

Shameless promotion

If you have a book you would like to get published and are not sure how you want to publish, I am available to consult with you and help you make the best choice according to your needs, your abilities, and your level of motivation. Contact me at Rik@PublishingSuccessOnline.com.

"Publication - is the auction of the Mind of Man."

- Emily Dickinson

New Book

"Publishing for Penny-Pinchers!"

Coming soon! It may even be here already, so check my website www.PublishingSuccessOnline.com or search for the title on Amazon or Barnes & Noble websites.

*"Every creator painfully experiences
the chasm between his inner vision and
its ultimate expression. The chasm is never
completely bridged. We all have
the conviction, perhaps illusory,
that we have much more to say
than appears on the paper."*

- Isaac Bashevis Singer

Glossary

Glossary

Acknowledgments – a list of people known to the author who have helped in the development and production of the book.

Adobe eBook – a book publishing concern. For more information go to: **http://www.adobe.com/digitalpublishing/ebook/**.

Appendix – an information section, usually added at the end of the book that contains additional material that did not fit easily into the main part of the book or it may be specific references for further inquiry.

Article – a short piece of writing usually between 250 and 3,000 words on a particular subject. Article submission guidelines are often listed on a publication's website.

Bar code – a scannable area usually placed on the back cover of a book that includes an ISBN (International Standard Book Number) and a price extension.

Benefits – the information contained within the book that solves a problem or reduces a pain.

Bibliography – a listing of the resources used as references in the writing of the book.

BISAC code – (Book Industry Standards and Communication) refers to the subject headings normally in the upper-left corner of the back cover, describing the most likely audience for your book. **http://www.bisg.org/what-we-do-0-136-bisac-subject-headings-list-major-subjects.php.**

Blog – or web log, can be a personal diary or a personal diatribe written and posted on the Internet. Blogs cover a wide variety of subjects from personal issues to commercial concerns, and everything in between.

Blurb – the incendiary headline and list of benefits placed on the back cover of a nonfiction book, with a call to action that gets customers to buy the book.

Book – in the age of technology a book can be a traditional hardcover, paperback, or an electronic book in several formats including Kindle, Nook, Google, iPad, etc. A book can also be a PDF file, an audio program, an MP3 file, and more as technology allows.

Chapter – a specific portion of a book that can be from one page to several pages long, usually containing information on a single topic area different from other parts of the book.

CIP or E-CIP – Cataloging-in-Publication or Electronic-Cataloging-in-Publication: is a distinct set of bibliographic information posted on the publication page of a book that contains the author's name, birth (and death, if applicable) dates, book description, topic areas, and a numerical code for shelving the books (Dewey system). Librarians appreciate CIP info. **http://cip.loc.gov/.**

Conclusion – has many similarities to a summary, but may also involve the writer giving their final opinion on a subject.

Contents – an outline-style listing of chapters, often with subheadings, to give a reader a good idea of what information is covered within the book.

Copyright – legal protection for any work that is recorded in writing, captured by audio, video, photographic, or other physical or electronic means. Copyright protection is not the same as copyright registration. For that, you will need to fill out Form TX electronically or physically to record your copyright. **http://www.copyright.gov/eco/.**

Cover – arguably, after the book title, the most important part of the book. A book cover or marketing image should convey to a potential buyer what the book is all about at first glance and even from a distance of 10-feet away. Spend the money to get a professional book cover designed.

Credits – a listing of copyrights and/or permissions acquired or required for elements used in a book, usually placed on the publication page.

Dedication – a "Thank You" to a very important person in the author's life, like a spouse or a mother. God forbid! Don't forget your mother.

Depository – with regard to articles is a place online that collects information from different authors. Examples are **http://hubpages.com/_signups/hub/funfamefortune** and **http://ezinearticles.com/** among many others.

Digital book – a book published in an electronic format, which can include eBooks, PDF files, books on eReaders, and audio files.

Edit – the process of proofreading, spellchecking, and correcting grammar and punctuation errors in a written document. There are several different forms of editing available beyond the basics described here.

End note – references placed at the end of a book rather than distracting footnotes on pages in the main body of the book.

Footer – the information contained at the bottom of each page independent of the other text on the page. Footers may include footnotes, references, page numbers, copyright notification, even contact information.

Footnote – a reference, usually denoted by a small number next to a word that indicates additional information on this element is located at the bottom of the page.

Foreword – often misspelled as "Forward," is a section where an author may have another person, such as a celebrity, comment about the book or the topic. Think extended testimonial.

Glossary – a listing of terms and their definitions used in a specific field or discipline.

Google books – a book publishing concern. For more information go to: http://books.google.com/intl/en/googlebooks/publishers.html.

Header – the information included at the top of each page independent from the page text. Headers can be page numbers, book titles, chapter titles, sometimes URL's, copyright information, and possibly graphic elements.

Illustration – an illustration could be a hand drawing, a picture, a painting, a symbol or icon, or a photograph. Always get permission to use an illustration before including it in your book!

Index – an alphabetical list of topics contained within the book always associated with their page numbers.

Introduction – where the writer says hello and invites the reader to enjoy the rest of the book.

ISBN – International Standard Business Number. An identifying code for books supplied by http://www.bowker.com/index.php/publisher.

Kindle – a book publishing concern. For more information go to: https://kdp.amazon.com/self-publishing/signin.

Link – a URL or Universal Resource Locator, usually light blue in color and underlined so that when clicked on, leads you to another website. Hypertext links or URLs may be listed in your book as further reference material for the reader.

LOC – Library of Congress. **http://www.loc.gov/index.html.**

Marketing image – the electronic version of the book cover. Books online do not normally include a spine or a back cover, so the front cover or marketing image must grab the reader's attention. Remember, the image should be clear, even at the thumbnail size, which is a common size for display on many eReaders. Also, keep in mind the eReader may present the cover in a black and white or grayscale image. Adjust your cover or marketing image accordingly.

Nook – a book publishing concern. For more information go to: **http://pubit.barnesandnoble.com/pubit_app/bn?t=pi_r eg_home**

Page break – used when you want to jump to the next page and continue typing in a document you are writing, whether you have filled the previous page or not.

Page number – mmm..., duh!

PCN – Pre-Assigned Control Number delivered by the Library of Congress when new authors register their books. **http://pcn.loc.gov/**

Permission – a written statement allowing you to use a quote, reference material, or illustration owned by another person (or company) in your book.

Photograph – a picture taken with some form of camera. All photographs require permission from the copyright holder (and sometimes the individuals pictured) before you can legally reprint the photograph in your book.

Preface – introductory remarks by the author that often provide an additional bit of information prior to the "Introduction" to put the reader in a proper mindset.

Price – the value placed on a product that (hopefully) results in a profit for the author after printing, commissions, and fulfillment fees are deducted.

Proposal – similar to a query letter, but provides more information, usually about a nonfiction book you would like to have published. A proposal may need a book outline, sample chapters, a book synopsis, and even a detailed marketing plan.

Publication page – usually appears on the reverse side of the title page. The publication page contains: book title, author, copyright information, publisher info, ISBN number, Library of Congress number, a disclaimer, CIP data, credits, and other publishing specific information.

Pull quote – a quote used like an illustration or graphic element (often set off by a text box) to emphasize some portion of the text.

Query – a letter to an agent or publisher detailing what your book is all about and why they should publish it.

Reference – a specific notation further defining some element of the writing, a publication, or a quote.

Release – permission received in writing that allows you to use a quote, extended amounts of writing, an illustration, a photograph, or any other element owned by another individual within your book.

Resources – books, websites, speeches, interviews, audio, or video used in the development of the book.

RF license – a RF license is a "royalty free" license allowing you to use a photograph in a specific way and for a limited number of times by paying a small fee for the license. RF licenses may differ according to each stock photo agency's guidelines.

Side bar – a unique story or additional information placed in a box to the side of the main story.

Spell check – is a function of many word processing programs to check the document for correct spelling. Spell check programs cannot tell the difference between words like their, there, and they're, and an incorrect word spelled correctly will not be brought to your attention. Always proofread your document.

Stock photography – A collection of photographs compiled for individuals to license for use on their websites, books, and in other presentation modes.

Summary – a condensation of all the information and facts presented in the writing.

Supporting Point – information that bolsters or expands a specific idea, usually from 250 to 500 words in length and written without regard to other elements of the chapter or book.

Testimonial – A brief two-to-three-sentence brag about your book. It can be written by family, friends, relatives, experts, celebrities, and (if you've been really good) Oprah! The dirty little secret of the publishing industry is that most testimonials are written by the publisher, the marketing department, or the author, then sent to a celebrity in question with a request for permission to print within the book.

Title page – can be the first page after the book cover or after a few pages of testimonials, which contains the book title, the author's name, and usually the name of the publishing company.

References:

Edwards, Betty. <u>Drawing on the Right Side of the Brain</u>. New York: Jeremy P. Tarcher / Putnam, 1989.

Bly, Robert W. <u>The Copywriter's Handbook: A Step-By-Step Guide To Writing Copy That Sells</u>. New York: Holt Paperbacks; 3rd edition, 2006.

Hill, Napoleon. <u>Laws of Success</u>. Chicago: Success Unlimited, Inc., 1979.

Krantz, Marshall. <u>Ideas and Research</u>. Cincinnati: Writer's Digest Books, 1996.

Parv, Valerie. <u>The Idea Factory</u>. St. Leonards, NSW, Australia: Allen & Unwin Pty Ltd., 1995.

Pearl, Luke. Be a Better Writer. <u>http://www.be-a-better-writer.com/creative-writing-quotes.html</u>

von Oech, Roger. <u>A Whack on the Side of the Head: How You Can Be More Creative</u>. Stamford: U.S. Games Systems, Inc., 1983, 1990.

The Quote Garden: <u>http://www.quotegarden.com/writing.html</u>

Resources / Links:

Consulting:

Rik Feeney – **www.PublishingSuccessOnline.com**

Brian Jud - **www.premiumbookcompany.com/**

Dan Poynter - **http://ParaPublishing.com**

Editorial:

Jan Green - **http://www.thewordverve.com/**

Jennifer Gregory – **jenniferediting@gmail.com**

Maureen Jung - **http://wordspringconsulting.com/**

Misty Powell - **mysti5d@gmail.com**

Transcriptionist:

Jan Green - **http://www.thewordverve.com/**

Writer's Organizations:

AuthorLink -
http://www.authorlink.com/conferences/writersorgs.php

American Society of Journalists and Authors -
http://www.asja.org/

National Writers Union - **http://www.nwu.org/**

Florida Writers Association - **http://www.floridawriters.net/**

Publisher's Organizations:

Independent Book Publishers Association –

http://www.ibpa-online.org/

Florida Publishers Association - **http://www.flbookpub.org/**

SPANnet - Self Publishing Information - **www.spannet.org/**

Small Publishers, Artists, and Writers Network -

www.spawn.org/

Online Publishing:

EzineArticles - **http://ezinearticles.com/**

Kindle - **https://kdp.amazon.com/self-publishing/signin.**

Nook-
http://pubit.barnesandnoble.com/pubit_app/bn?t=pi_reg_home

Google -
http://books.google.com/intl/en/googlebooks/publishers.html

Hubpages - **http://hubpages.com/**

Scribd - **http://www.scribd.com/home**

Smashwords - **https://www.smashwords.com/**

YouPublish - **http://www.youpublish.com/**

POD Publisher:

Booklocker.com - **http://publishing.booklocker.com/**

Richardson Publishing – **www.PublishingSuccessOnline.com**

Stock Photography:

BigStockPhoto - **http://www.bigstockphoto.com/**

Dreamstime - **http://www.dreamstime.com/**

Getty Images - **http://www.gettyimages.com/**

istockphoto - **http://www.istockphoto.com/**

Writer's Conferences & Workshops:

Shaw Guides - **http://writing.shawguides.com/**

Ordering Information

To order copies of this book, or other books by Rik Feeney, please visit:
www.PublishingSuccessOnline.com
or visit online sites like Amazon.com, BarnesandNoble.com, etc.

For gymnastics books written by Rik Feeney, please visit:
www.GymnasticsTrainingTips.com

About the author

Rik Feeney adapted his love of reading, writing, and gymnastics to become a published author of more than 48 books, reports, and CDs on the sport and business of gymnastics, as well as a book coach, author web page designer, and promotional expert for aspiring authors.

Rik received a Bachelor of Arts in Writing & Literature from Vermont College of Norwich University in 2003. He is currently a columnist for AllExperts.com, answering questions in two categories: Publishing and Self-Publishing and the sport of Gymnastics.

He currently works with authors and self-publishers as a book development and marketing coach, providing insight and information to help new writers leap beyond the mundane but financially treacherous concerns of traditional publishing.

He is also the Orlando Florida Writer's Association group leader, hosting monthly meetings at the University Club in Winter Park.

A funny, provocative, and knowledgeable speaker, Rik Feeney has presented at many writer's conferences and seminars and is constantly working on new books.

Email Rik at **Rik@PublishingSuccessOnline.com** or visit his web site at **www.PublishingSuccessOnline.com.**

Rik's Blog:
http://www.publishingsuccessonline.com/blog/

CPSIA information can be obtained
at www.ICGtesting.com
Printed in the USA
LVOW12s1652100416

482935LV00001B/2/P

9 781935 683155